There Is A River

There is
a river
whose
streams
make glad
the city
of God.

Psalm 46:4

Spirit Talk

MESSAGES

Reverend Paula J Behrens ®

Devotional Messages

July - December 2010

There Is A River

Other books in the *Spirit Talk collection*:

Walking In the Light
Grace to You
Blessed Are the Peacemakers
If You Love Me
Goodness & Mercy
Praise the Name of the Lord

Reverend Paula J Behrens is a full membership Elder in the Texas Annual Conference of the United Methodist Church, Ordained in 2007. She graduated from *Houston Baptist University* with a *Bachelor of Arts* degree in Christianity and English and acquired her *Master of Divinity* from *Perkins School of Theology*, Southern Methodist University.

Reverend Behrens has served as pastor in six United Methodist congregations. She is currently appointed as the Senior Pastor of Chappell Hill United Methodist Church in Chappell Hill, Texas. She has three grown children and three grandchildren. Her desire is to use her gifts and graces in such a way as to bring as much glory to God's kingdom as possible in this lifetime.

Her desire is to use her gifts and graces in such a way as to bring as much glory to God's kingdom as possible in this lifetime.

This collection of messages is lovingly
dedicated to my children:
Sharleen Manning
Bruce Behrens, Jr.
Nicholas Behrens

My siblings:
Cathy Behrens
Bobby Acree
Sylvia Thomas

And the members of:
Chappell Hill United Methodist Church
5195 Church Street/ PO Box 285
Chappell Hill, TX 77426
(979) 836-7795
www.chappellhillumc.org

There Is A River

Table of Contents

SCRIPTURE INDEX

OLD TESTAMENT

Numbers 21:4-9
Jeremiah 31:31-34
Amos 7:7-17

NEW TESTAMENT

Matthew 1:18-25
Matthew 24:36-44
Mark 2:13-22
Mark 4:35-41
Mark 5:21-43
Mark 6:1-6
Mark 6:1-13
Mark 10:2-16
Mark 12: 28-34
Luke 1:39-45
Luke 2: 8-20
Luke 6:17-26
Luke 15: 1-3, 11b-32
Luke 22:14-20
John 1:1-14
John 6:1-21
John 12:20-33
Ephesians 1: 1-14
James 3:13-18; 4:7-8*a*

Preface

There once was a little girl who attended church only because her parents dropped her and her siblings off for Sunday school and worship every week. Now, this was a good thing, because at least she did have a chance to hear about the love of God. But it was not the best thing, because her parents never joined them for worship and that influenced how she thought about God.

What happened is this little girl grew up thinking that church was only for children. And she reasoned, just as soon as she was grown, well, she wouldn't have to go to church any more. And that's exactly what happened, once she was grown, she did as her parents had done, dropping her own three children off for Sunday school and church, and seldom attending herself. It was her understanding that she was an adult and adults didn't need anyone's help (not even God's). She could and would take care of herself.

She had been taught that if she just worked hard enough, she would be able to get all the things she needed, all the things that would bring happiness and contentment into her life. It might take a while, she thought, but she could do it. And so she worked very hard at acquiring all the things she needed and all the things she wanted, and by the age of forty she had most all of them: a nice house, a faithful husband and three beautiful children.

But guess what, she wasn't happy, she wasn't content. At her dismay, she sensed that there was something missing. She didn't quite know what it was, but she knew something was missing. It seemed that there was this strange emptiness in her life. It was like she had a hole in her heart.

Later she would find out that that is the way our Creator made each of us, with a "God shaped hole" in our hearts. Later she would find out that her life was plagued with a human condition that goes all the way back to the beginning of time. Later she would find in her quest for self sufficiency that she had moved away from the One who created her, that she had become separated from God.

This book, a part of a collection called *Spirit Talk* came about through a little girl's personal journey with God, her journey from unbelief into belief, from something that was less-than-life (as God intended it to be for her) to Life that was "very good" in God's eyes.

Very good, in the first two chapters of Genesis, we hear that it was *"in the beginning that God created"* the world, the cosmos, and everything in it, including human beings, and God saw that it was "very good." We also hear that the first couple (Adam and Eve) walked with God, well that is, until they decided to listen to a crafty old serpent instead. The first couple was given, by God, the ability to make choices, and that day by the tree of "Knowledge and of Good and Evil," they made a not so good choice, which spiritually separated them from the One who had created them. Just like the little girl, the first couple found themselves separated from the One who had created them. They made a choice, and people have been making choices every since that day, some good and some not so good.

For example, there was the prodigal son who chose to leave his father. You might have heard the story. In Luke 15:11-24 there were two sons, one who thought it unfair that his father would throw a party for his irresponsible little brother. And another who was called a prodigal.

According to the dictionary, the word "prodigal" means "recklessly wasteful." It is derived from a Latin word, which is translated "to squander." Therefore, a prodigal son is literally a wasteful son, one who throws away opportunities recklessly and wastefully.

The younger son in this famous parable is a waster. He is one of the most famous wasters in the entire Bible. Now, in our imaginations we can read between the lines and pencil in all the sordid ways he must have wasted his inheritance.

He had a good case of the "give-mes." "Give me the share of the property that will belong to me," he said. He takes the money and blows it on "dissolute living." We know this story well. We know all about this prodigal, this waster. And what we don't know, our imaginations are more than happy to provide.

And we know all about the father, too, who takes back his wayward son even before the confession gets completely confessed. The father runs across the field and smothers his son with hugs, a robe, a ring, and a huge party. But, we have to ask ourselves: Why did the prodigal come back?

Well, he began to feel that emptiness in his heart. He knew that something was missing. He realized that he needed that relationship with his father. The scriptures tell us: *"He came to himself."* You know, it's just a fact that God created us for a living relationship with Him (our heavenly Father). And no matter how much we acquire, or how much we achieve, nothing (can replace that personal relationship with God) nothing can satisfy our soul, nothing, not money, or sex, or power, nothing. God knows that.

Have you ever noticed that the central theme of the Bible is the story of God calling us back into that relationship with Him? It is. Jesus called people to accept the relationship God offers them. In Matthew 11:28 we hear Him saying: *Come to Me, all you who are weary and are carrying heavy burdens, and I will give you rest.*

You see, God offers to us, not a system of rules, but a personal relationship with Him. And with that relationship comes a mysterious and wonderful grace, justifying grace, which begins to work the moment we say "yes" to God. And, our acceptance changes everything. In the story of the prodigal, justifying grace begins when the younger brother turns away from his misery and returns home.

Luke 15: 20-24 says: *So he set off and went to his father. But while he was still far off, his father saw him and was filled with compassion; he ran and put his arms around him and kissed him. And the father said in His joy get the fatted calf and kill it, and let us eat and celebrate; for this son of mine was dead and is alive again; he was lost and is found! And they began to celebrate.* His broken relationship with his father was amazingly restored. And that's what it is like for those of us who believe (but it is even better). Through, belief in Jesus Christ, we are restored to an Eternal relationship with God.

Using the analogy of human courtship, when we accept God's grace, we say "yes" to the One who has been wooing and pursuing us. And as in courtship, saying "yes" changes the nature of the relationship completely. For a husband and wife, saying "yes" marks the beginning point of a lifelong commitment to marriage and a shared life. And this commitment (is meant by God) to resemble our eternal commitment to Jesus Christ and His mission.

But, even though a person responds in faith, it can only be done because of God's grace. The apostle Paul confirms that as he writes in Ephesians 2:8-9: *For by grace you have been saved through faith, and this is not your own doing; it is the gift of God -- not the result of works, so that no one may boast. It is only by grace that you have been saved through faith*.

Another interesting fact about salvation is this. It is instantaneous and continuous (all at the same time). It is correct to say: *I was saved* by grace, *I* am *saved* by grace, and *I will be saved* by grace. In scripture, this spiritual experience of justifying grace is known by several names: salvation, healing, conversion, having one's sins forgiven, or being born again.

And now, as Paul Harvey would say: Here's the rest of the story. The little girl I was telling you about earlier, the one who thought church, was just for children, the one who was on a self sufficient quest for happiness, well that little girl was me. You see, I had chosen the path, the wide path that taught: This life is all there is and you are in charge of making it good. I truly believed that this life was my only chance for happiness. And in my misguided understandings I assumed that after this earthly life, a person just simply ceased to exist.

And because of my childhood experience as a church "drop-off kid," I really didn't even believe that there was a God. And of course if I didn't believe there was a God why in the world would I believe that there was a Heaven or a Hell? It just didn't make sense to me. And so, when you think about all of that, well, it's really not surprising that I didn't come into a saving relationship with Jesus Christ as a child or even as a young adult. The most amazing thing though, is this: God waited patiently, He waited for forty years, for my heart to be ready for the miraculous change that He had in store for His little girl.

I remember it well. I was sitting at the desk in the game room of our 4200 square foot home. And I was feeling that empty feeling in my heart. And I began to pray, really pray, for the first time in my life, I began to pray as though there might just possibly be someone out there to hear me.

I begin by praying: God, if You are really out there, and at that moment God brought back to my memory a verse of scripture that I had learned as a child. It was the verse in Matthew where Jesus says: *Come to Me, all you who are weary and are carrying heavy burdens, and I will give you rest.*

And I said: God, if it is really true that I can have that rest and that peace that Jesus says I can have, I want Him in my heart. I want to give my life to Him. And at that moment my heart was changed.

The way that I saw God, the world around me, other people, and myself was completely different. And as I sat there thinking, I said to myself: Now, I didn't bargain for that. I didn't even know that my heart could or even needed to be changed like that. And then a light bulb came on in my mind.

As the logical thinking person that I am, I realized that I didn't change my heart, but my heart was definitely changed. And I had to ask the question: Well, who did that? If it wasn't me who changed my heart, who did that? Then I realized, that it was something outside of myself that had changed my heart.

And at that moment, I realized that God was real! I began to experience a Joy and Peace and Contentment, like I had never experienced before. I was filled with an unquenchable desire to read the Bible and would do so, two and a half times in the next four months. I also, began to feel a tug on my heart to serve as a pastor in God's church.

Now, I can't tell you that it was easy, no in fact it was quite the opposite, I would say. It was a twelve and a half year journey from call to ordination. But amazingly God was there for me the whole way, strengthening me, encouraging me and carrying me when need be.

And to make a long story short: This *Spirit Talk* collection of books is one small part of my journey with God, one that I wanted to share with you, in hopes that the Lord will take my small offering, multiply it and use it for His glory. And so, here goes. Following you will find a collection of messages that were preached in Chappell Hill, Texas during the second half of 2010. It is my prayer that you might be able to glean a little nugget of God's grace and peace as you incorporate these messages into your walk with Him.

Blessings,
Paula Behrens

Freedom

<u>Mark 6:1-6</u>
He left that place and came to his hometown, and his disciples followed him. On the sabbath he began to teach in the synagogue, and many who heard him were astounded. They said, "Where did this man get all this? What is this wisdom that has been given to him? What deeds of power are being done by his hands! Is not this the carpenter, the son of Mary and brother of James and Joses and Judas and Simon, and are not his sisters here with us?" And they took offense at him. Then Jesus said to them, "Prophets are not without honor, except in their hometown, and among their own kin, and in their own house." And he could do no deed of power there, except that he laid his hands on a few sick people and cured them. And he was amazed at their unbelief. Then he went about among the villages teaching.

When the pilgrims came to America, it took them 23 years to pay for their own passage. They were blown 500 miles off their course, and so they didn't land in Virginia; they landed in Massachusetts. But when they finally stood on that rocky coast, they fell down on their knees and kissed the earth, and they wrote for all of history to find: "We establish this state to the glory of God and the spread of the Christian religion."[1] The United States certainly was not the first experiment in democratic government. That had been tried twenty centuries earlier in the Greek City States, and failed. No, there was only one thing that made America an experiment that was unique in the pages of history. It was a Christian democracy. There was only one thing over the years that held this nation together, only one thing! I challenge you to mention another. One thing, we were a nation under God, and we knew it.

That was the dynamic. That was the inspiration. That was the goal of the experiment. It was a simple axiom. Lose that force, and you lose the nation. Lose that Power and this country, as we have known it, will be gone.

The American experiment was no selfish enterprise, either. It was an example for the whole family of humankind. If we are the mightiest nation on earth, and we are, then this is the mission of the mighty, to carry freedom to all people. We will never be truly or safely free until all people on earth enjoy that same freedom. This I believe.

Let us pray: May the words of my mouth and the meditations of each of our hearts be acceptable in Your sight, O God, our Rock and our Redeemer. Amen.

"Except in his own hometown... a prophet has honor," Jesus said. And it's no wonder. Prophets speak to a people on behalf of God. But here's the question: What nation on earth has ever lived up to God's standards without Him? Not us. Not Israel. Not any nation that has ever existed on earth. We need to remember the importance of God as we continue to celebrate our grand, national holiday this weekend.

You know, I'm thankful to be an American. Nevertheless, the Fourth of July is a dangerous day. Not because of fireworks, reckless driving, swimming accidents and such. It is a dangerous holiday because the celebration can blind us to certain temptations in America. Today we will look at three. The first temptation of Americans is to enjoy the fruits of citizenship without tending the tree of Liberty. Harry Emerson Fosdick preached a sermon years ago called, "Parking on Another Man's Nickel." And the idea is still sound, today. You come to a parking place that has a meter. Happily there is still time on the meter. This must be your lucky day. You pull in and park on someone else's nickel, or quarter or whatever.

But, Fosdick went on to say that, sadly enough, some of us go all through life parking on someone else's nickel. We forget that along with freedom, comes responsibility, civic responsibility. Is our community a better community because we live in it? Our state? Is the PTA stronger because we have a child in school, a grandchild? Can the local nursing home count on our support? How about the Hospice resale shop? These are not glamorous questions. These are simply the nuts and bolts of citizenship. Are you parking on someone else's nickel? The first temptation is to neglect the tree of Liberty, civic responsibility.

The second temptation of the American people is to neglect the tree of Justice, to want someone else to take care of the poor among us. But, taking care of the poor, is the responsibility of the church. It is not the responsibility of someone else. When the church turns its responsibility for the poor, over to someone else, chaos happens. Yet, that is where we are headed today. Jay W. Richards, the author of the book, Money, Greed, and God, writes: Our governments "War on Poverty" cost trillions of dollars and didn't work. Like poison fruit our federal welfare system the one designed to help the disadvantaged, ended up rewarding destructive behavior instead. As Aristotle said twenty-five hundred years ago, "If you want to encourage something, reward it. If you want to discourage it, punish it." If women are given more aid if they have more children with unknown fathers, but cut off punished if a father is around, you can be pretty sure you'll end up with a lot of children without fathers and a lot of women as wards of the state. The government is too large to see what is best for the people, but the church, God wisely planted the church within the community where we can see the needs of an individual. God has a plan to help the poor among us, and that plan is to be carried out by His church. We can give a helping hand, through things like after school tutoring programs, or computer training for young parents, or offering a course in Home Economics, or parenting classes, or DivorceCare.

We could even get the community involved by inviting people in to help, bag and send rice and beans to feed hundreds, possibly thousands of starving families in other countries. By offering a hand-up instead of a hand-out, the church can help to restore dignity to a people who have been told that they have no skills to do anything good. The church is small enough to help others be self sufficient and better equipped, to enter into the business world and large enough to feed thousands, not only physically, but also spiritually as God's love flows through His church and out to the world. Some people, even some well meaning Christians, have justified government programs, by quoting Jesus' story about a man who falls into the hands of robbers. They compare the wounded man to the poor, and the Good Samaritan to the government.

But, if you look more closely at the story you will see that the Good Samaritan was an individual who gave of his own money to take care of the wounded man. This was not a government program caring for the poor, but one individual helping another out of the goodness of his heart. The problem isn't that government workers are uncaring. The problem is all about information and incentives. The church is close to the problem, the government is not. Plus, government programs tend to make the people they serve, slaves to the system. The worst part is this, people on federally sponsored hand-out programs begin to look to the government for their daily provisions, instead of God. In reality, the government becomes their provider and their false god, which robs us of our freedom under God, and enslaves us as a people under an impersonal governing authority.

And the reason this is happening in America is because there is confusion among us. For example, in the book of Acts when the Holy Spirit first descended upon the early church we hear that: *The whole group of those who believed were of one heart and soul, and no one claimed private ownership of any possessions, but everything they owned was held in common.*[2] Some who read this passage wonder if the Christian ideal isn't communism or socialism.

Well, on the surface it might look similar to communism or socialism. But it is not. First of all, unlike modern communism, there's no talk of class warfare, nor is there any hint that private property is evil in some way. These Christians are selling their possessions and sharing freely and spontaneously. And also, the state is nowhere in sight. No government is confiscating property. No one is being coerced. The church in Jerusalem was just that, the church, not the state. The church does not act like a modern communist state. No one in the book of Acts gets their stuff confiscated; sharing was voluntary, not compulsory. Christian sharing is always voluntary sharing that comes from the heart.

Yet some still say: Well, you know, maybe socialism is better. I mean, after all doesn't capitalism and free enterprise spawn greed within a persons' heart. Well, no, actually, it does just the opposite. Listen to Richards as he quotes Adam Smith, saying: Capitalism is fit for real fallen, limited human beings. "In spite of their natural selfishness," business people "are led by an invisible hand, and thus without intending it, without knowing it, advance the interest of the society." He then continues to explain how free enterprise can actually transform the thinking of a self-centered person. In this example, it is a butcher. Richards writes: Even if the butcher is selfish, even if the butcher would love nothing more than to sell you spoiled, beef in exchange for your worldly goods, the butcher can't make you buy his meat in a free economy. He has to offer you meat you'll freely buy. The butcher, in other words has to look for ways to set up win-win scenarios. Even to satisfy his greed, he has to meet your desires. The free market makes this happen. That's making the best of a bad situation, and of a bad butcher. Free enterprise encourages win-win scenarios as a self-centered person begins to look outside himself.

Here's something else to think about. The American way of dealing with the economy creates wealth for poor and not so poor, alike. Think about the farmer who has a small plot of land and is just barely able to support his family. He tills the soil, plants the seeds, harvests the crops and sells the excess for a profit. That is what farmers have been doing for centuries. But, human beings are created to be creative. What if this farmer uses his creative ability to paint scenic pictures of the farm around him and sells the pictures in the marketplace with his vegetables? That's the beauty of free enterprise, through his willingness and creativity he is able to increase his wealth; the poor does not have to stay poor.

The rewards of working creatively, encourages small business men and women to pursue their visions as they seek to create something that will fulfill some need or desire, a stirrup that makes it easier to ride horses, a nut that tastes good when it's toasted, mashed and spread out on bread; adhesive that's sticky enough to post a note but not too sticky, so you can remove it when you're done; cat litter that makes it easy to keep your cat indoors. Free enterprise is God's plan. I think it is God's plan for human beings to be creative, in the image of their Creator.

Free enterprise also lines up with the biblical work ethic. The apostle Paul knew this when he wrote: *"Anyone unwilling to work should not eat."[3]* Work is a good thing. Work itself is part of Gods' original blessing; it is not a curse after the fall. Work came before the fall when God told man to "till the earth and tend to the garden."[4] John Wesley, the founder of Methodism, once said: "Earn all you can. Save all you can. And give all you can." Christians living in a free society, who are able to work and make a profit are better able to give "all they can" to others in need. And they do this, like Wesley, out of a desire that is placed in their heart through the work of the Holy Spirit, not because someone or something forces them to.

Jesus was never about force. God never uses force, not even when it comes to His own people loving Him. Which, brings us to our third temptation, side-stepping the tree of Faith, that of wanting Christianity without conversion. What I am talking about here is the luke-warm claim of faith that some people in the church make because it seems to be the right thing to do. But instead, what is truly required is a level of intense commitment to Jesus Christ, the same kind of commitment seen in the hearts of our founding fathers and mothers. True faith in Christ is much more than a mere intellectual assent. What I am talking about is belief with the heart and with the will that results in worship of God and action for Him. Those who have experienced true faith in Christ will understand the importance of not side-stepping the tree of Faith.

Let me ask you this. How much difference does it make in your life to say, "Jesus is Lord"? You know, God is not so much about fixing things that have gone wrong in our lives as He is about finding us in our brokenness and giving us Christ. When Christ is not central and supreme in our lives, everything about life shifts out of orbit and moves out of kilter. So for Christians, our first task is to know Jesus. And out of that knowing, we will come to love Him, adore Him, proclaim Him, and manifest Him.[5]

Lots of responsibilities come with living in America, one nation under God, indivisible, with liberty and justice for all, but it is worth the effort. The tree of Liberty (civic responsibility), the tree of Justice (offering a hand-up), and the tree of Faith (true Christian conversion), none of these can be neglected if we wish to continue in freedom. That is God's will and that is our mission. We've got work to do, and it won't be an easy task. But it will be possible, because we live in a nation where we can still say: "In God we trust!" Amen.

Who Me?

Amos 7:7-17

This is what he showed me: the Lord was standing beside a wall built with a plumb line, with a plumb line in his hand. And the LORD said to me, "Amos, what do you see?" And I said, "A plumb line." Then the Lord said, "See, I am setting a plumb line in the midst of my people Israel; I will never again pass them by; the high places of Isaac shall be made desolate, and the sanctuaries of Israel shall be laid waste, and I will rise against the house of Jeroboam with the sword." Then Amaziah, the priest of Bethel, sent to King Jeroboam of Israel, saying, "Amos has conspired against you in the very center of the house of Israel; the land is not able to bear all his words. For thus Amos has said, 'Jeroboam shall die by the sword, and Israel must go into exile away from his land.'" And Amaziah said to Amos, "O seer, go, flee away to the land of Judah, earn your bread there, and prophesy there; but never again prophesy at Bethel, for it is the king's sanctuary, and it is a temple of the kingdom." Then Amos answered Amaziah, "I am no prophet, nor a prophet's son; but I am a herdsman, and a dresser of sycamore trees, and the LORD took me from following the flock, and the LORD said to me, 'Go, prophesy to my people Israel.' "Now therefore hear the word of the LORD. You say, 'Do not prophesy against Israel, and do not preach against the house of Isaac." Therefore thus says the LORD: 'Your wife shall become a prostitute in the city, and your sons and your daughters shall fall by the sword, and your land shall be parceled out by line; you yourself shall die in an unclean land, and Israel shall surely go in away from its land.'"

There's a store-front church which is called Almighty God Tabernacle. One Saturday evening, the pastor of this church was working late, and decided to call his wife before he left for home. It was about 10 PM, but his wife didn't answer the phone. The pastor let it ring about two dozen times but she didn't answer. He thought it was a little odd, but decided to try a few minutes later. When he tried again, she answered right away. He asked her why she hadn't answered before, and she said that the phone didn't ring. They brushed it off as a fluke and went on their merry ways.

The following Monday, the pastor received a call at the church office, which was the phone that he'd used that Saturday night. The man that he spoke with wanted to know why he'd called on Saturday night. The pastor couldn't figure out what the guy was talking about. Then the guy said: "It rang and rang and rang, but I didn't answer." The pastor then remembered the mishap and apologized for disturbing him, explaining that he was trying to call his wife. The man said: "That's okay. Let me tell you my story. You see, I was planning to kill myself that night, but before I did, I prayed, 'God if you're there, and you don't want me to do this, give me a sign now.' At that point my phone started to ring. I looked at the caller ID, and it said: 'Almighty God and I was afraid to answer!'"[6] The things that God does and the ways that He does them are, many times, a mystery to us. That's probably what the prophet Amos was thinking when God called on him to take God's message of doom to Israel.

Let us pray: May the words of my mouth and the meditations of each of our hearts be acceptable in Your sight, O God, our Rock and our Redeemer. Amen.

Amos went from the farm where he talked with the animals and dressed the trees, to proclaim to a nation and its king that they needed to mend their ways. His call and his credentials were not from any connection with the professional prophets, but from God alone. A more unlikely prophet could scarcely be found.

And, even today, God chooses to call some very unlikely people into His service. I, personally, am far from being a shining star of a preacher, but the fact that I do it at all is unusual, to say the least. When God called me into the ministry I had never even heard of a woman preacher. I came from a family of farmers and construction workers. I was terrified to speak in public. And so, the fact that I love what I do now is something of a miracle in and of itself.

How about you? Did you ever once think you would one day sing in the choir, that you would teach a Sunday school class, that you would lead a women's or men's group, or sit on a church board and be a part of a decision making group for the whole church? Did you ever dream, before you came to Christ, that you would be one who fearlessly witnessed for Him and tried to live your life as He directed? Maybe, you were an unlikely candidate too. Maybe, one day, while you were "tending sheep and dressing trees" or selling cruises, or managing a company, or preparing tax forms, or building a house, or tending to the front desk of a large company, or pleading a court case, or whatever, God called you. And however unlikely it seemed, the glad result is that here you are doing exactly what God called you to do.

The truth is that fundamental qualities for ministry are within the reach of every consecrated person. God doesn't require those He calls to be intellectual scholars, or extraordinary in any other way. But, He does demand, that a person have a virtue that is sweetened by the spirit of Jesus Christ. The spiritualization of our average capacities is much more important than the possession of unusual gifts. Our ordinary abilities, when touched by the Spirit of God, become extraordinary. Isn't that great? But, why do you think God does that, letting us use our ordinary talents for Him? And what kind of job profile do you think He uses as He selects appropriate candidates?

Well, I'll give you a little help. There seem to be three characteristics of the kind of people God chooses, according to our prophets' story this morning. First of all, you've got to be willing to lay down your life. Now, I'm not talking about martyrdom, though that could happen. I'm talking about laying down your life, your dreams, your deepest, desires. Someone once said: "Man is looking for better methods; but God is looking for better men and women." That's true. God is looking for men and women, and boys and girls, who are willing to live their life in the center of God's will.

The French Foreign Legion had this motto: If I falter, push me. If I stumble, pick me up. If I retreat, shoot me. Suppose that kind of commitment were required in order to be used of God. Would you qualify? God is looking for people who are willing to lay down their life, their own personal dreams, and deepest desires, for what, for God's agenda. That is the first characteristic God looks for in those He uses. And the second is this: God looks for people who are single-minded in their devotion.

But, you know what? Unlike Amos there are many people who want to live for their selves and not for God. Now, they don't mind dabbling in religion, after all, a little bit is good for you. But they would never dream of focusing everything they are and everything they have on that one magnificent obsession. On the other hand, Amos had the single-minded devotion that God looks for in His servants. His cause was righteousness and justice. And regardless of how the people of Israel resisted his prophecies, Amos was not deterred. He was not a people pleaser, but a God pleaser. *"The Lion has roared,"* Amos declared, *"Who will not fear? The Lord God has spoken, who can but prophesy,"* he said.[7]

A timid minister, who often straddled the fence, was told by one member of his congregation to preach the "old-fashioned gospel" and was instructed by another member to be "broad-minded." And as a people pleaser, instead of a God pleaser, the result of his struggle was evident in his next sermon.

He said: Unless you repent, in a measure, and are converted, so to speak, you are, I am sorry to say, in danger of hell-fire and damnation, to a certain extent. You know, God doesn't like fence-sitters, not knowing who they should please, people or God. But Amos was not a fence-sitter. No, he came speaking: *"thus saith the Lord"* with boldness and with conviction. Amos was single-minded in his devotion to God, as we all should be.

God calls people who are willing to lay down their lives. God calls people who are single-minded in their devotion. And finally, God calls those who understand the difference between the temporal and the eternal. If we live for today and this life and think there is nothing more, then perhaps it is understandable that we have little concern for righteousness and justice. But if there is something more, if there is a righteous God who has created this world and loves it and who seeks the welfare of all of its people, then our willingness to order our lives according to His principles is quite important.

Israel was living for its own pleasure, and so, the message that Amos had to deliver, was that of God's imminent judgment on them. And it would not be just a mere slap on the wrist to warn them, this time, but it was the ominous word of almost total destruction of the nation. The unthinkable was about to happen to Israel. That was and still is God's message to a wayward nation. God would uproot his people for their sins and lack of repentance, and He would do it by the hands of a pagan nation. But still, even so, unbelievable as it seemed, if they would repent, if they would repent and turn their hearts back to God then God would have mercy on the remnant. He would not wipe them out completely. It is as if God had a love affair with his people and even when they deserted Him, and were unfaithful to Him, and disobedient to Him, He found it hard to let them go.

The great magician, Harry Houdini, had a lifelong love affair with his wife. He was always writing her little notes. They always began: "Dear Bess, You'll never know how much I love you."

She said that, long after his death, she was still finding those notes, in the attic, in the office, in pockets, and under things. How like God that is! He could not, He would not, forsake His people if there was even a glimmer of a chance of their returning to Him. They had been warned over and over, again and again they had been exhorted to repent. And no matter what kind of punishment He sent to them now, they would deserve it. They had sinned beyond all the limits of Divine compassion, but, unbelievably, God's great promise came to them. God said: *If you repent... I'll restore the kingdom, the house of David will rule once more over Israel and you will feast on wine and fruit in the promised land.* God's love for His people is beyond human comprehension. And so, it only make sense that we who have experienced that Love, God's Love, that we, too, should respond with a similar type of love for others.

You know, the only thing we can take with us to the next world is that which does not consist of physical matter, our kindly deeds, the love we have shown, and the things we do for Christ, as we seek to serve Him. *Whatever you do, in word or deed, do everything in the name of the Lord Jesus, giving thanks to God the Father through Him,* the apostle Paul told the believers at Colossi.[8] A remarkable lady named Minnie Pearce had the lead in the senior play during her college days. She worked hard on the part, and after the performance she was startled when a strange man came up to her backstage and introduced himself as the author of the play. He said, "I just wanted to come back and tell you that I have seen this drama many times, but tonight you embodied what I envisioned for the lead character better than anyone else ever has. Tonight, you made a dream of mine come true; you gave my play flesh and blood and I want to thank you."[9] We can only ask ourselves the question: Wouldn't it be wonderful to get to the end of the drama of this life, and there to meet the Divine Author, and have Him say: "You made the dream I had for you come true! What I had in mind when I created you is exactly what you did with your life's days and nights!"

You know what? God's definition of success is very different from the world's definition of success. It really doesn't matter how smart we are, how talented, or how successful we are in the eyes of other people. It's only what God has in mind for you and me that matters. So here it is. God is looking for people who are willing to lay down their lives, people who are single-minded in their devotion to Him, and who understand the difference between the temporal and the eternal. And, we still have a chance; we still have a chance to get it right, to repent, to obey, and to claim the eternal promises of God. That's my goal, to get life right for God. It should be yours, too. Amen.

Who's the Prodigal?

<u>Luke 15: 1-3, 11b-32</u>
Now all the tax collectors and sinners were coming near to listen to him. And the Pharisees and the scribes were grumbling and saying, "This fellow welcomes sinners and eats with them." So he told them this parable: Jesus said, "There was a man who had two sons. The younger of them said to his father, 'Father, give me the share of the property that will belong to me.' So he divided his property between them. A few days later the younger son gathered all he had and traveled to a distant country, and there he squandered his property in dissolute living. When he had spent everything, a severe famine took place throughout that country, and he began to be in need. So he went and hired himself out to one of the citizens of that country, who sent him to his fields to feed the pigs. He would gladly have filled himself with the pods that the pigs were eating; and no one gave him anything. But when he came to himself he said, 'How many of my father's hired hands have bread enough and to spare, but here I am dying of hunger! I will get up and go to my father, and I will say to him, "Father, I have sinned against heaven and before you; I am no longer worthy to be called your son; treat me like one of your hired hands."' So he set off and went to his father. But while he was still far off, his father saw him and was filled with compassion; he ran and put his arms around him and kissed him. Then the son said to him, 'Father, I have sinned against heaven and before you; I am no longer worthy to be called your son.' But the father said to his slaves, 'Quickly, bring out a robe-- the best one--and put it on him; put a ring on his finger and sandals on his feet. And get the fatted calf and kill it, and let us eat and celebrate; for this son of mine was dead and is alive again; he was lost and is found!' And they began to celebrate. "Now his elder son was in the field; and when he came and approached the house, he heard music and dancing. He called one of the slaves and asked what was going on. He replied, 'Your brother has come, and your father has killed the fatted calf, because he has got him back safe and sound.'

Then he became angry and refused to go in. His father came out and began to plead with him. But he answered his father, 'Listen! For all these years I have been working like a slave for you, and I have never disobeyed your command; yet you have never given me even a young goat so that I might celebrate with my friends. But when this son of yours came back, who has devoured your property with prostitutes, you killed the fatted calf for him!' Then the father said to him, 'Son, you are always with me, and all that is mine is yours. But we had to celebrate and rejoice, because this brother of yours was dead and has come to life; he was lost and has been found.'"

One Religious Ed teacher was reading the story that we just heard about the prodigal Son to his class, clearly emphasizing the resentment the older brother expressed at the return of his brother. And when he was finished telling the story, he asked the class, "Now who was really sad that the prodigal son had come home?" Then after a few minutes of silence, one little boy raised his hand and confidently stated, "The fatted calf."[10]

Let us pray: May the words of my mouth and the meditations of each of our hearts be acceptable in Your sight, O God, our Rock and our Redeemer. Amen.

We live in a world where the concept of fairness is so important to so many people. And if you are, or have been around children much, then you will recognize that most childhood squabbles erupt from a very old emotion; that of feeling somehow slighted or mistreated. He got more of that special ice cream than I did. No fair! Why does she get to stay up a half-hour later than I do? That's not fair! He got to sit in the front seat last time. It's not fair that I always have to sit in the back. Her curfew is 12:30. Why do I have to be home at midnight? And if you think we outgrow this obsession with fairness, think again.

I've seen adults argue over something as simple as their place in line at Wal-Mart. Today we heard about two sons, one who thought it unfair that his father would throw a party for his irresponsible little brother.

According to the dictionary, the word "prodigal" means "recklessly wasteful." It is derived from a Latin word, which is translated "to squander." Therefore, a prodigal son is literally a wasteful son, one who throws away opportunities recklessly and wastefully. The younger son in this famous parable is a waster. He is one of the most famous wasters in the entire Bible. Now, in our imaginations we can read between the lines and pencil in all the sordid ways he must have wasted his inheritance. He had a good case of the "give-mes." "Give me the share of the property that will belong to me," he said. He takes the money and then blows it on "dissolute living." We know this story well. We know all about this prodigal, this waster. And what we don't know, our imaginations are more than happy to provide. And we know all about the father, too, who takes back his wayward son even before the confession gets completely confessed. The father runs across the field and smothers his son with hugs, a robe, a ring, and a huge party.

But, there's also a second son, an older son who has been working his fingers to the bone all day. Or, make that all month, because he's been doing his own work plus that of his brother for weeks now. He is exhausted, his boots smell of cow manure, and he could certainly use a shower. And then he hears it, music and dancing. The Greek word here for "music" is interesting. The older brother hears the symphonia. Not just a fiddle and a banjo player. He hears a "symphony" of instruments, an orchestra of merriment. And he is confused until someone finally breaks the news to him, a robe, a ring, and a fatted calf, an unbelievably excessive trinity of welcome for someone who's been a royal pain in the neck. *"Father, give me the share of the property that will belong to me,"* said the younger son before he left.

So tell the truth. Had you been in the older brother's shoes, working double shifts while your, younger brother lived it up, would you have gone into the party? Be honest. There is something primitive and basic afoot here that tweaks our sense of moral outrage. And I'll tell you why, it simply wasn't fair.

There are many theological nuggets to mine in this story. But this is perhaps the most basic one: God isn't fair. Sorry. God doesn't play by our rules, see life the way we see it, or keep score the way we keep it. God isn't fair. God isn't fair. And not only that: God loves the sinner, not the sin, but the sinner. He throws a party of rich food and drink to get their attention. He slips a ring on their finger and kills the fatted calf for them. And where does the parable end? Are we inside the party celebrating? Or are we standing outside with our arms folded with the older brother, refusing to go in? That's where Jesus leaves it. He doesn't tell us how the story will end. The father passionately invites the older son inside, "pleads with him" to join in the welcome. Curiously, however, we are never told what the older brother decides to do. The story ends but it doesn't end. You can almost hear the voice of Walter Cronkite saying, "You Are There." Will you RSVP to a party thrown by an unfair God? Or will you stubbornly remain outside?

In a world where God does not play fair, this parable forces us to make a choice and ask: Who is the real "prodigal" here? Who is the real "waster?" From the beginning Jesus says that this is a story about two brothers. Which one is the authentic prodigal? Which one has yet to come home to the Father's extravagant love? You know, we can waste our lives keeping score and complaining about unfairness. We can harbor grudges until we die. We can completely misunderstand what Jesus is all about even as we worship every Sunday. We can waste life waiting for apologies, waiting for people to act decently and fairly, waiting for others to earn our forgiveness and acceptance.

But, Jesus waited on none of those things. As I recall, His words as they nailed his hands and feet to a cross were: *"Father, forgive them; for they know not what they do."[11]*

You know, every Sunday God throws a party for sinners. Some have recently been in a "far country" and are making their way back home. And others have been working hard in the fields of the Lord for years. And they, like the older brother, have slipped into a religion that is more about controlling God's love, rather than celebrating it. And, there have been a lot of older brothers in the history of the church. We, United Methodists certainly know about the older brother, because their own John Wesley was the best of them. He was so earnest, so methodical about his devotional life that people called him a Methodist and the name stuck. But it was not until his 35th year, when he was at Aldersgate, that Wesley experienced God in such a way that he was able to write: I suddenly felt my heart strangely warmed. I felt that Christ had died for my sins, even mine and had saved me from the law of sin and death. Wesley had never gone to the far country. But he needed to know how much God loved him too. He needed to feel some excitement about his religion. He needed a homecoming party.

And then there is Simon, You may remember the story. Jesus was invited to the home of this remarkable man. Simon was a rare and loyal Pharisee who was so much like the older son in so many ways. Simon never left the Father's home. And one afternoon he invited Jesus to dine with Him. While they were eating Jesus was suddenly approached by a woman of the streets who came crying and begging for His forgiveness. And this display of emotion was embarrassing for Simon. Jesus said: Let me tell you a story. There was a man who had two debtors. One owed him 50 days of work and the other owed him 500 days of work. Neither could pay so the man cancelled the debts of both of them. Now, which one will love him the most? And Simon responded: *"Why, of course, the man who was forgiven the 500 days of work debt."*

Simon gave the right answer to Jesus' question but I wonder if Simon really understood the underlying meaning. The one who owed 500 days of work was obviously the woman. But the one who owed the 50 days of work was Simon himself.

So, let me ask: Because Jesus forgave the woman a bigger debt does that mean that Jesus loved her the most? No. Because in the end He forgave them both didn't He? And also, now listen to this, in actuality He forgave them both the same amount because He forgave them all that they owed. And that's the important thing here. Most of us are like the older son in that we think God must certainly measure sin. We think that in the end some people will owe more than others. But I want to tell you that it doesn't make any difference whether you owe God 50 days of work or 500 days of work, you can't pay it. It doesn't make any difference whether you're an inch outside the Kingdom or a mile outside the Kingdom, you are outside the Kingdom until you receive forgiveness and come in. The older brother needs a Savior just as much as the younger brother. The older brother is just as much a prodigal in his behavior as the younger brother. If the older brother had just realized that bitterness must be left outside the party and forgiveness must enter in, if Simon had rejoiced at this woman's repentance and forgiveness, it would have made all the difference in the world.

So who is the real prodigal? Well, it's not the one with a shady past. It's the one who stays outside, the one who cannot bring himself to forgive. The father said: *"This brother of yours was dead and has come to life; he was lost and has been found."* The one we usually call "prodigal" is alive. Found. That means the dead one, the lost one, is the one who stubbornly chooses to remain outside the Father's party. What a waste. What a waste.

Now, if we were honest, we would have to admit that our churches today are probably full of older brothers and sisters. And as a result many Christians are living as though they don't even have a Father. They earnestly do what earnest people ought to do, but their souls are not aglow.

How about your soul? How is it with your soul today? Are you going to be like the older brother, standing outside the door of God's kingdom? Or are you going to come in and celebrate the redemption God offers to you, through Jesus Christ? The door is open and the Father is pleading with you. Won't you come in, and receive His forgiveness today? He is waiting for you. In the name of the Father and of the Son and of the Holy Spirit. Amen.

Take This Bread

<u>Luke 22:14-20</u>

When the hour came, he took his place at the table, and the apostles with him. He said to them, "I have eagerly desired to eat this Passover with you before I suffer; for I tell you, I will not eat it until it is fulfilled in the kingdom of God." Then he took a cup, and after giving thanks he said, "Take this and divide it among yourselves; for I tell you that from now on I will not drink of the fruit of the vine until the kingdom of God comes." Then he took a loaf of bread, and when he had given thanks, he broke it and gave it to them, saying, "This is my body, which is given for you. Do this in remembrance of me." And he did the same with the cup after supper, saying, "This cup that is poured out for you is the new covenant in my blood.

Jesus took bread, and when He had given thanks He broke it and gave it to His disciples saying: *"This is My body which is given for you. Do this in remembrance of Me."*

Let us pray: May the words of my mouth and the meditations of each of our hearts be acceptable in Your sight, O God, our Rock and our Redeemer. Amen.

At Passover time in the springtime of the year AD 30, little clusters of Jewish men, women and children gathered all over the city of Jerusalem to do what their ancestors had done for nearly thirteen centuries. They shared a meal together. Now, every Jewish meal was a religious occasion. Their meal began with a father, a rabbi, or a host, taking bread into his hands, and saying: *Blessed art thou, O Lord our God, King of the universe, who brings forth bread from the earth.*

Then, the entire meal would follow. Cups of wine were taken during the meal. And at the end of the meal, there would be the final cup of wine called "The Cup of Blessing." Again, the father, the rabbi, or the host would take the cup of wine and this time he would say: *Blessed art thou, O Lord our God, King of the universe, who creates the fruit of the vine.* Jesus did this every time He sat down with His twelve disciples. On Thursday night, before Good Friday of what we now call Holy week, Jesus did what He had done many times before. He took bread, He gave thanks, He broke the bread, and He gave it to His disciples at the beginning of the meal. This time, however, He did something He had never done before. At the beginning of the meal, He identified the bread with His body. And at the end of the meal, He took the Cup of Blessing and said something He had never said before. As He gave them the cup, He said: *"This is my blood of the new covenant. Do this in remembrance of Me."[12]*

Whenever Jewish people kept the Feast of Passover, they kept it as a way of remembering. In the Book of Exodus, we hear: *For seven days you shall eat unleavened cakes, and on the seventh day there shall be a pilgrim-feast of the Lord. On that day you shall tell your son or daughter, "This commemorates what the Lord did for me when I came out of Egypt."[13]* The Jewish Passover was a way for each Jew to remember God's great act of deliverance. But on that Thursday night, on the night Jesus would be betrayed. Instead of saying: *"Do this in remembrance of what the Lord did when we came out of Egypt,"* He instructed: *"Do this in remembrance of Me."[14]* And so, when Christians, to this day share in Holy Communion, we are instructed to remember another great act of deliverance, that of God's deliverance for us through Christ, Jesus.

We hear Paul in his second letter to the Corinthians speaking for Christ and saying: *"This is My body that is for you... And this cup is the new covenant in my blood. Do this, as often as you drink it, in remembrance of Me. For every time you eat this bread and drink the cup, you proclaim the death of the Lord, until He comes."[15]*

When we partake of the sacrament we are reminding ourselves, of what Christ did for us. We are also remembering the fact that our Lord will return. Throughout the Old Testament, remembering played a powerful role in the history of the people. And they had different physical reminders to help them with this. Physical reminders help us to remember, as well. And they also play a part in stirring the memories of other people around us.

For example there was once a little girl who thought her mother was the most beautiful woman in the world, except for one thing: Often, she would say to her mother: "I love the beauty of your face and your eyes and your hair. But, thank God that you wear gloves, because I can't stand to look at your hands. They are so scarred and ugly." Finally, her mother said to the little girl: "Let me tell you what happened. When you were a little baby, a fire broke out in our house. I ran up the stairs and through the flames to your room. I picked you up and carried you out of that burning house. From that time on, my hands have looked like this." After that, those scars became a thing of beauty and a continual memorial for that little girl. Her mother's hands became a symbol of her great love for her. Likewise, the Lord's Supper continually reminds us of the sacrifice that was made on the Cross for us, but there is much more.

Holy Communion is not only a remembrance of what Christ did for us in the past, but it is also, a celebration of what He is doing for us now, in the present. We believe that Christ Himself comes to us in this sacrament. When we gather at His table, we believe that Christ is our host. As we take this Bread and drink from this Cup, in repentant faith, Christ comes to give us forgiveness of sins, new life and eternal salvation. Holy Communion is something that God does for us. He comes with forgiveness of sins. He brings assurance of salvation. He gives strength for battling temptation and enables us to live the abundant life. Psalm 55:22 says: *"Cast your burdens upon the Lord and He will sustain you."*

Many of us become burdened with worries, concerns, and problems, of this life. But, in Holy Communion, Christ invites us to come to Him, so that He can relieve us of our burdens, and give us instead, a wonderful assurance of God's presence with us, and His forgiveness. Christ is present in this Holy meal, in a mysterious and unexplainable way. Through this meal we are relieved of our burdens, that is if we will allow God to work that mystery within us.

But, the trouble is that, many times, we refuse to trust God enough to cast our burdens on Him. Too many of us choose to hold on to our burdens as we add today's pain onto yesterday's sorrow and top it all off with worry about tomorrow. So many of us have not learned the tremendous lesson that Jesus taught in the Sermon on the Mount when He said: *"Do not worry about tomorrow for tomorrow will have worries enough of its own."*[16] God wants us to trust Him to be present with us and then to just live one day at a time.

In her book <u>Nestle, Don't Wrestle</u>, Corrie ten Boom tells an old, Dutch parable about a clock that had a nervous breakdown. The clock had just been finished and placed on the store shelf with two older clocks on either side. One was an old table top clock which was very negative about life. To the new young clock, he said: "So, you're just starting out in life. I feel sorry for you. Just think for a bit and see how many ticks lay ahead of you. You'll never make it! You'd better stop now." And the new little clock took the advice and began counting the ticks: "Let's see, each second requires two ticks which means 120 ticks per minute, 172,800 ticks per day; 1,209,600 ticks per week for fifty-two weeks - and that makes a total of 62,899,200 ticks in a year! Oh no!" said the new clock and then he had a nervous breakdown and stopped ticking.

On the other side was a wise old mantel clock who overheard the conversation. She chimed in and said: "You silly youngster, don't listen to all his negative comments. He's been unhappy for years and wants you to share his misery. Think about it another way. How many ticks do you have to tick at one time?" The new clock replied: "Only one, I suppose." "That's right!" said the mantel clock. "That's not so hard is it - just one tick at a time. And one more thing, don't ever think about the next tick until you have finished your last one." Soon the new clock was running smoothly - just one tick at a time.

This morning we have the opportunity to sit at the Table with our Lord, one more time. And we will break bread together as we share the sacrament of Holy Communion. So, let's each make a commitment, that as we take the Bread and the Cup, we will trust God as we live just one day, one tick at a time. Let's not permit our pain, our burden of sin, or our worries to mount up. Instead let's cast all those things into the hands of Him who loves us, Jesus Christ our Lord. He can give us rest and He can renew our strength, as we are willing to lay down our burdens at the foot of His cross. And as we come to His table this morning, we need to remember that Jesus will be present, in a special and mysterious way, celebrating with us. He is not here to change the bread and wine into His body and blood. And He is not here simply to help us remember his great sacrifice for us on the Cross. But, Jesus is here to forgive us, to strengthen us, to save us, and to love us. He is here inviting us, saying: "Come to Me, My heavy laden children and I will give you rest. Cast your burdens upon Me and I will sustain you."

During this very special meal, I hope that you will be able to believe, to trust that Christ is present with us this morning. And I hope that you will confess your sins to Him, and hear Him say: "You are forgiven." Place all your cares, fears, worries and burdens at the foot of His cross, and know that He will strengthen and sustain you. Then leave this place refreshed, renewed, rejoicing, and ready for a brand new life in Christ. Amen.

He Met Them On Level Ground

<u>Luke 6:17-26</u>
He came down with them and stood on a level place, with a great crowd of his disciples and a great multitude of people from all Judea, Jerusalem, and the coast of Tyre and Sidon. They had come to hear him and to be healed of their diseases; and those who were troubled with unclean spirits were cured. And all in the crowd were trying to touch him, for power came out from him and healed all of them. Then he looked up at his disciples and said: "Blessed are you who are poor, for yours is the kingdom of God. "Blessed are you who are hungry now, for you will be filled. "Blessed are you who weep now, for you will laugh. "Blessed are you when people hate you, and when they exclude you, revile you, and defame you on account of the Son of Man. Rejoice in that day and leap for joy, for surely your reward is great in heaven; for that is what their ancestors did to the prophets. "But woe to you who are rich, for you have received your consolation. "Woe to you who are full now, for you will be hungry. "Woe to you who are laughing now, for you will mourn and weep. "Woe to you when all speak well of you, for that is what their ancestors did to the false prophets.

Jesus died penniless. And His only possessions, the clothes on His back, Roman soldiers cast lots for them to divide them. Jesus died hungry. There is no record that Jesus had anything to eat the day of His death. What we call the Last Supper on Thursday evening may very well have been Jesus' last meal. He died on the cross Friday with an empty stomach. Jesus died weeping. After His last supper Jesus headed for the Garden and there in that Olive Grove we call Gethsemane He prayed and He wept.

Jesus died hated. Caiaphas, the greatest religious authority in Israel called Him a blasphemer. The crowds wanted a murderer freed before they would see Jesus pardoned.

Before all of this happened, Jesus looked up to His disciples and said: *"Blessed are you who are poor, for yours is the kingdom of God. Blessed are you who are hungry now, for you will be filled. Blessed are you who weep now, for you will laugh. Blessed are you when people hate you, and when they exclude you, revile you, and defame you on account of the Son of Man. Rejoice in that day and leap for joy, for surely your reward is great in heaven."*[17]

Let us pray: May the words of my mouth and the meditations of each of our hearts be acceptable in Your sight, O God, our Rock and our Redeemer. Amen.

The beatitudes from our reading today, are a wonderful description of what Jesus was like and what His disciples were called to be like. Blessed are the poor. Blessed are the hungry. Blessed are those who weep and are hated. They sound so spiritual, don't they? And they probably come in fourth in the "framed scripture hanging on a wall category." Just behind The Ten Commandments, the Twenty-third Psalm and the Lord's Prayer. But if the truth be told, even if we hang them on our wall, few of us probably ever come close to truly living them out. Because they are such a strong call to sacrificial living.

When it comes to making sacrifices, E. Stanley Jones was perhaps Methodism's most famous foreign missionary. He wrote over a dozen books and converted hundreds of Hindus in India to Christianity. And he is the only person, I think, who was voted in abstentia to become a bishop. And when he received the news, he turned it down. One day Jones came to Emory University and spoke to a Systematic Theology class. One of the students asked him why he turned down the appointment as bishop. And he laughingly replied that if he became a bishop he would have to retire at age 70. "I am now 82," he said, "and I am still going strong."

Then someone asked him: what do you think of the Beatitudes? Several students picked up their pens expecting something profound, and they got it. Here's what he said: "At first sight, you feel they turned everything upside down. On second thought, though, you understand that they turn everything right side up. The first time you read them they seem impossible. The second time you read them, when you realize they turn everything right side up, nothing else is possible.

Now, the beatitudes are not a chart for Christian duty, he continued. Instead, they are a charter for Christian liberty." In other words, they set us free to be what God created us to be. The Beatitudes: This is where Jesus met His disciples on level ground. This is where He met them with admonitions of sacrificial living, which is the door to Christian Freedom.

Let's take a closer look. First, Jesus puts in a good word for poverty, hunger, and sadness. Interesting isn't it? We have been conditioned all our lives to work hard, build wealth, and provide for our families. But these beatitudes turn all of that around. Look carefully at what takes place in this text. There are two small points that are easily missed. The first is that Jesus turns away from the crowd and speaks directly to His disciples. The second is that Jesus does not say: "Blessed are the poor," which is the way most of us quote it when we quote it from memory. No, listen carefully, Luke quotes Jesus, saying: "Blessed are you who are poor." He is talking to His disciples. They are the ones who have become poor. They are the ones who have worked day after day without food. Remember the story about Jesus and the disciples walking through the grain fields on the Sabbath? Matthew, in chapter 12, tells us this story because he was there. He says the disciples were hungry so they began to pick some heads of grain. Have you ever been so hungry that you ate raw grain right off the stalk?

The disciples, I am sure, wept on occasion and they were hated by many because of their allegiance to their Lord. The Beatitudes then are not instructions on how to live. They are commendations, kudos, congratulations, for how the disciples were already living. They left family and home to serve with Jesus and He was proud of them. He says to them: Blessed are you twelve for you have given up your careers and become poor to serve with Me.

Now, that understanding is what makes this passage difficult to preach on. Because it brings to our attention how short we Christians in America have fallen. The Beatitudes address a very strict and sacrificial way of living that is very difficult to attain, at least, in our own strength. But, if there was an example of a modern day disciples sacrificing their life it would have to be Mother Teresa. Some years ago before she died, a television special depicted the grim human conditions that were a part of her daily life. It showed the horrific conditions of the slums of Calcutta and her love for these destitute people. The producer interviewed her as she made her rounds in that dreadful place. Throughout the program commercials interrupted the flow of the discussion.

Here is the sequence of the topics covered and then the commercials. Lepers (bikinis for sale); Mass starvation (designer jeans); Agonizing poverty (fur coats); Abandoned babies (ice cream sundaes); The dying (diamond watches). The irony was so apparent. Two different worlds were on display, the world of the poor and the world of the affluent. It seems that our very culture here in the United States, and any other place that has a great deal of commercialization, is teaching us that the only way a person can be blessed, is to be materially rich. I mean, we are occasionally presented with the images of the poor but we never are tempted to assume that life style. Think about it. And so, it is shocking to read Luke's Beatitudes as an admonition to live unencumbered by worldly wealth, isn't it?

But as soon as we are reminded that Jesus calls us to sacrificial living we are immediately reminded of the next purchase we should make, or the next meal we should eat. We are slowly and systematically told that the best way to live our life is in luxury.

But it is not so in the Kingdom of God. This was not the attitude of the first disciples. How can we reclaim the Beatitudes? How can we hear them over the Super-bowl halftime shows and million dollar commercials? It's not easy. I am a small voice here and there are only you out there in the pews. But Jesus had fewer still. He turned away from the crowd and spoke only to His disciples. So I speak to you today: Blessed are you who are poor for yours is the kingdom of God. Blessed are you who give, who do without, who sacrifice. Let's put in a good word for being poor, hungry and sad. Let's put in a good word for sacrificial living.

Second, Jesus cautioned His disciples against riches, food, and worldly happiness. Frederick William the fourth, of Prussia, once visited a school and quizzed the students. He held up a stone and asked the children: to what kingdom does this belong? They responded: mineral. He then, pointed to a flower and asked: to what kingdom does this belong? They answered: plant. He then pointed to a bird flying by outside the window and asked: to what Kingdom does that belong? They replied: animal. Then he asked: Now, to what kingdom do I belong? To what kingdom do we belong? Now, in a scientific sense, we are of course, part of the animal kingdom. I belong to the same kingdom as my new little kitty cat, Cali. And Cali is like other pets I have had, she has many human traits. She can pout; she can get excited; she has a temper. Yet, Cali does not understand time. She cannot grasp that there is a point beyond which she will not live. Only humans can grasp time. Her limited mind cannot set goals. Cali cannot tell right from wrong. It is not within her to share. It is not within her to sacrifice for another. All of those are human traits.

The magnificent thing for humans is that it is within us to rise above the animal kingdom and become a part of another kingdom, the Kingdom of God. Jesus is appealing to our human nature. Appealing to the most unique thing on this planet, the human capacity to love and sacrifice for a cause greater than ourselves. Will I be only of the animal kingdom, and take care of myself, or will I be more fully human and take care of others? Will I be rich in this life or poor here adding richness to the next life? Will I fill my stomach or go without, adding satisfaction to the life to come? Will I live for the moment or do the hard work of sacrifice, which may bring some discomfort in the here and now, but will yield heavens worth of joy in the next? What does my discipleship look like when I compare it to the Beatitudes? That's the question.

And finally, we learn that sacrificial freedom is greater than financial freedom. Tell me: What brings happiness, wealth or poverty? Ken Hubbard said: "It's pretty hard to tell what does bring happiness. Poverty and wealth have both failed." Well, if that is the correct answer, maybe we should ask a different question. Maybe we should rather ask, what brings meaning to life? Martin Luther, the Priest who brought about the Reformation had the answer, he said: A Christian is the most, free person of all, and subject to none; a Christian is the most dutiful servant of all, and subject to everyone. This was his definition of Christian Liberty. Listen again: A Christian is the most, free person of all, and subject to none; a Christian is the most dutiful servant of all, and subject to everyone. To be poor in Jesus' mind is to be free from the entanglements of the world and therefore free to serve in the Kingdom of God. That's what brings meaning to life. As we go through life it's easy to miss what is significant, though, isn't it?

One pastor, Leith Anderson, shared an experience. As a boy, he grew up outside of New York City and was an avid fan of the old Brooklyn Dodgers. One day his father took him to his first major league game. It was a World Series game between the Dodgers and the Yankees.

He was so excited, and he just knew the Dodgers would stomp the Yankees. Unfortunately, the Dodgers never got on base, and his excitement was shattered. Years later he was engrossed in a conversation with a man who was a walking sports almanac. And he told him about this World Series game he attended as a boy and added: "It was such a disappointment. I was a Dodger fan and the Dodgers never got on base." The man said: "You were there? You were at the game when Don Larsen pitched the first perfect game in all of World Series history." And he replied: "Yeah, but uh, we lost." He then realized that he had been so caught up in his team's defeat that he missed out on the fact that he was a witness to a far greater page of history.[18]

Let me ask you a question. What's going on down the street in our ballpark? We may be so caught up in the beauty of our building, the eloquence of the sermon, and the friends who sit around us, that we miss out on a far greater page in the story of our Christianity. Look around you. What is it that is happening in our community? What is it that is happening down the street at your neighbor's house? What is happening over in the schoolyard in Brenham? What is happening on campus at Blinn College? Is God pitching a perfect game in the world series of our neighborhood and we simply are missing out because we are too invested in our own local congregation?

Jesus met His disciples on level ground that day and that's where we find ourselves today, as well. Jesus said to His disciples: Blessed are, you who are poor, hungry, weeping and hated. Blessed are you because to you belongs the Kingdom of God. I wonder how He intends for that to be played out in our lives today. You know, the Beatitudes address a very strict and sacrificial way of living that is difficult to attain, at least, in our own strength. But then, we are reminded of this magnificent fact: All things are possible through Christ who strengthens me, and you, and all who know Him personally. Now, that's something worth thinking about. Amen.

Peace in the Storm

Mark 4:35-41

On that day, when evening had come, he said to them, "Let us go across to the other side." And leaving the crowd behind, they took him with them in the boat, just as he was. Other boats were with him. A great windstorm arose, and the waves beat into the boat, so that the boat was already being swamped. But he was in the stern, asleep on the cushion; and they woke him up and said to him, "Teacher, do you not care that we are perishing?" He woke up and rebuked the wind, and said to the sea, "Peace! Be still!" Then the wind ceased, and there was a dead calm. He said to them, "Why are you afraid? Have you still no faith?" And they were filled with great awe and said to one another, "Who then is this, that even the wind and the sea obey him?"

Victor Hugo, author of the famous novel, the Hunchback of Notre Dame also wrote a story called "Ninety-Three." It's about a ship that is caught in a dangerous storm at sea. At the height of the storm, the frightened sailors hear a terrible crashing noise below the deck. And they know at once that the noise is from a cannon, part of the ship's cargo, that has broken loose. It was crashing into the sides of the ship as it swayed back and forth in the storm. Knowing that it could cause the ship to sink, two brave sailors volunteered to make the dangerous attempt to retie the loose cannon. Why? Because they knew the danger from inside the ship was much greater than the danger caused outside the ship by the storm.[19] And, if you think about it, that's the way life is, too. The storms of life may blow around us, but it's not those exterior storms that pose the greatest danger. No, there is a more dangerous storm that can come from within.

Let us pray: May the words of my mouth and the meditations of each of our hearts be acceptable in Your sight, O God, our Rock and our Redeemer. Amen.

The furious storms outside may be overwhelming but what's going on inside can pose an even greater threat to our lives. That's what the disciples learned that day on the Sea of Galilee. They thought the danger was outside the boat, but they would soon learn that the real danger was within the boat, within their own hearts. In a word, they lacked faith. And without faith their lives were at risk when the storms would inevitably come. And come they did.

So, our question today is: What can we learn from this boat ride in the storm? Well, first, we learn that storms can come suddenly. It had been a memorable afternoon for the disciples. People from all over had gathered to hear Jesus tell them about the Kingdom of God. He told them that the kingdom was like a farmer who went out to sow seeds. He compared the Kingdom to a small mustard seed, which becomes a giant plant. He told many stories, but the day was almost gone and it was time to leave. So, He told His disciples to go over to the other side of the Sea of Galilee. Now, surely the disciples must have wondered why Jesus wanted them to leave at that time. It seemed that they were right on the verge of something good with all the people gathered there. On the other side were only Gerasenes, unbelievers. But they did as Jesus told them, anyway. They set sail that beautiful afternoon on the Sea of Galilee. The sun was shining and Jesus, weary from the day's activity, fell asleep.

But as the late afternoon faded into dusk, trouble began. The white puffy clouds that dotted the sky were replaced by threatening black ones. The stilled waters began to churn with white caps, and then large waves slammed against the side of their tiny boat. And even though the Sea of Galilee was notorious for these sudden and violent storms, the disciples must have wondered if Jesus was leading them to their destruction, rather than their salvation.

You know, trouble can come just that fast in your life and my life, as well. Everything can be going beautifully. People can be congratulating you. Things can be going your way. Then all of a sudden the telephone rings and everything in your life is turned upside down. Maybe it's happened to you when your medical test came back, and all of a sudden you found yourself in the midst of a storm. Or maybe one of your children had gotten into some kind of trouble. No, it doesn't take long for the storms to come. Storms can come suddenly. The disciples experienced it and that's when they went to the stern of the boat where they found Jesus asleep. He didn't even know that a storm was raging. He couldn't even hear the howl of the wind. He didn't even feel the waves crashing into the side of the boat. Didn't He care? *"Teacher, don't you care if we drown,"* they asked? Doesn't God care about what I am going through? Doesn't God care about what you and I are going through? The sudden furious storm outside may seem overwhelming, but what we need to focus on is what is going on inside our lives. Who will calm the tempest? Who will calm the storm saying: *"Peace, be still"?*

First, storms can come suddenly and second, they can make you lose direction. That's another important lesson we can learn from this boat ride in the storm. We can lose our direction in a storm. It happened to the first disciples. Several of them were experienced fisherman. They had charted those waters hundreds of times before. They had been caught in many storms before: so, why all the fear this time? They begin chastising Jesus for not pulling His own weight. They find Him asleep and they say: *"Teacher, don't you care if we drown?"* In other words: Are You just going to sleep there or are You going to get up and help? Get up and grab an oar Jesus; we need all hands on deck. It's at this moment that the unexpected happens. Jesus gets up, and He doesn't grab an oar, but instead, He calms the storm. And that's why the disciples were terrified. Look at the story. The disciples are certainly frightened by the strength of the storm. They need everyone to pitch in but Jesus rebukes the storm, saying: *"Peace! Be still!"*

The disciples are stunned. They were looking for human help. But what they got was divine authority. They were looking for a hand. But what they got was a God. They were terrified and asked each other: *"Who is this? Even the wind and the waves obey Him!"*

Let me ask you, which is more powerful, the storm or the One who masters the storm? It was in the storm that the disciples lost their faith, as seen in Jesus' question: *"Do you still have no faith?"* They don't know who it is that rides in the boat with them. *"Do you still have no faith? Do you still not understand who I am,"* Jesus asks. They were frightened during the storm but after the storm they were filled with an awesome fear. Why? Because of He who was in the boat with them. Their real problem was not the storm outside but the storm of doubt and unbelief on the inside. They thought the danger was outside the boat, but then they realized that the real danger was within their own hearts. In a word, they lacked faith.

There was once a woman who was well known in her community for her simple faith and great calm in the midst of many trials. Another woman who had never met her but had heard of her came to visit one day. "I must find out the secret of her calm, happy life," she thought to herself. As she met her she said: "So you are the woman with the great faith I've heard so much about." "No" came the reply. "I am not the woman with the great faith, but I am the woman with the little faith in the great God."[20] Unlike the disciples, this woman did have some faith, little faith she called it, yet still some faith. In other words, what really matters is not the size of our faith, but the fact that we do have it, that we do have faith, in the Greatness of our God.

Where do you turn in the midst of the storm? It's an urgent question. It is a theological question, for sure, where do you place your loyalty?

A little girl was about to undergo a dangerous operation. Just before the doctor administered the anesthetic, he said: "Before we can make you well, we're going to have to put you to sleep." And the little girl responded: "Oh, if you are going to put me to sleep, then I have to say my prayers first." And at that, she folded her hands, closed her eyes, and said: "Now I lay me down to sleep, I pray the Lord my soul to keep. If I should die before I wake; I pray the Lord my soul to take. And this I ask for Jesus' sake. Amen."[21] Sometimes the Lord calms the storm. Sometimes He lets the storm rage and calms His child.

I do not believe that Jesus, in the boat that day, rebuked the disciples for their lack of faith in His ability to calm the storm, so much, as He rebuked them for their lack of faith in who, He was. If they understood that, then they would not have feared the storm. When you find yourself in the midst of a storm and the boat is sinking, may I suggest that you turn to Christ, immediately? Where else can you go for the help that you need? Only Jesus has the words of Eternal life. Only God is the Holy One. Only Jesus can calm the tempest. Only God can deliver.

And that brings us to our third and final point. If we do not understand, who it is in the boat with us, then fear has the power to paralyze us. When Jesus awakened, He rebuked not only the storm, but also, the disciples. *"Why are you afraid,"* He asked. *"Have you no faith?"* Now, let us be clear about this. The promise that is made to us is that of God's presence, no more, no less. In the midst of the storm, God will be in the boat with you. Jesus may not care about the storm. But He does care about us, who are in the storm.

This morning, it is easy for us to sit here in our air-conditioned sanctuary and think good thoughts about the world. But, you know, life can be tough. There can be darker, more difficult days than this. In this beautiful month of August, sitting on the front porch or walking in the park or just enjoying the scenery driving along a country road, the world seems benevolent and benign.

But this story of Jesus and His disciples in a boat gives us a better glimpse of the world we live in, a world where storms rise up out of nowhere and nature can put us in danger. That's what our reading is about today. Perhaps you thought that there would be smooth sailing with Jesus. Perhaps you thought that, with Jesus in the boat, there would be no storm, no waves and no fear. But, almost every page of Mark's gospel proclaims that Jesus is at the center of a storm. When Jesus is near, the wind picks up, the waves bang against the side of the boat, and there is trouble. You need not panic, though. The Lord of the Church is in the boat with you. You need not forsake your witness. The Lord of History is in the boat with you. You need not become paralyzed. The Lord of the storm is in the boat with you. That's the promise.

Will the clouds dissipate immediately? No guarantee. Will you no longer have to struggle with problems? That's not promised. Will you henceforth prosper, as the T.V. ministers assure you? Probably not. Well, you might say: That doesn't sound so great. Well, perhaps not. But it got Noah through the storm. It got the Israelites through the wilderness. It got Mary through her pregnancy. It got Jesus through the crucifixion. And it will be sufficient to get you through the storms as well. Why? Because Jesus who promises to be with you, Jesus the Peace at the center of the storm, is in the boat with you. So, do not fear. Just have faith. Amen.

What to do... When Rejected

<u>Mark 6:1-13</u>
He left that place and came to his hometown, and his disciples followed him. On the sabbath he began to teach in the synagogue, and many who heard him were astounded. They said, "Where did this man get all this? What is this wisdom that has been given to him? What deeds of power are being done by his hands! Is not this the carpenter, the son of Mary and brother of James and Joses and Judas and Simon, and are not his sisters here with us?" And they took offense at him. Then Jesus said to them, "Prophets are not without honor, except in their hometown, and among their own kin, and in their own house." And he could do no deed of power there, except that he laid his hands on a few sick people and cured them. And he was amazed at their unbelief. Then he went about among the villages teaching. He called the twelve and began to send them out two by two, and gave them authority over the unclean spirits. He ordered them to take nothing for their journey except a staff; no bread, no bag, no money in their belts; but to wear sandals and not to put on two tunics. He said to them, "Wherever you enter a house, stay there until you leave the place. If any place will not welcome you and they refuse to hear you, as you leave, shake off the dust that is on your feet as a testimony against them." So they went out and proclaimed that all should repent. They cast out many demons, and anointed with oil many who were sick and cured them.

Have you ever heard of Choglit soda or OK soda? Maybe you remember Surge, which was around for a few years and tasted a lot like Mountain Dew? No? Well, all three of these sodas were launched by Coca-Cola and all three were complete failures.

And about that, CEO E. Neville Isdell reminded shareholders, "As we take more risks, failures like these are something we must accept as part of the regeneration process."

Many big businesses are starting to recognize the importance of "intelligent" or "smart" failures. These failures might hurt in the short-term, but they offer critical lessons for long-term growth. It is significant to note that the long-term lessons would never be learned without taking risks in the short-term. In other words, sometimes that one step back is exactly what is needed to take a leap forward.[22] Jesus took that one step back, the day He went to His own hometown and was rejected. Because of the hard-heartedness of His own people, He was rejected. The townspeople said: *"Is not this the carpenter, Mary's son?"* which implied: *"Who does He think He is anyway?"*

The story begins with rejection and ends with the amazement of Jesus *"at their lack of faith."[23]* Let's take a closer look. The hometown people rejected Jesus. They did not accept Him, even in the Synagogue. The moment Jesus appeared to read and speak, it seems like the place became a noisy hall. Where'd He get all this? If that's who I think it is, why He is the one who helped build our house. Oh, yes, He made our furniture. I am sure He is the one who repaired my plow. I know His family. His brothers and sisters, His relatives are all members of this Synagogue. He used to sit beside us here in these pews. Hey, we can't have this! Maybe Jesus was tempted to give up on those people. The scriptures do tell us that *"He was amazed by their unbelief."*

You know, the book of Hebrews says that Jesus experiences all the temptations of humankind. Think of it. There is no temptation of which we could ever go through that Jesus did not experience. He knows them all, from the inside. That was the Apostle Paul's point too, when he spoke about a *"thorn in his flesh."[24]* *"I asked the Lord about it three times,"* Paul says. *"But He said to me: 'My grace is sufficient for you, for my power is made perfect in weakness.'"*

You see, that is what real humility is about, living by grace, living by the power of God in the weakness of our own bodies with all their limits. That's what humility before God is about. And God showed the way. God became a carpenter named Jesus, He took on human form. Was Jesus taken aback by the rejection He met with in His home town? Was He upset? Was He shocked? I am sure He was. But was He defeated? No. Even though He may have felt immobilized for a little while, He was not defeated.

What was the secret to the manner in which He handled it? Why was He able to move ahead, unaffected by this rejection, continuing to make Himself available to others? Well, He must have understood that His task was God-given. "I must give it a good trial," He probably thought. "Whatever it takes to do the job, I will do it," He told Himself. "Even if people reject me, I will refuse to waste my energy in anger and self-pity. I'll keep moving on. Somewhere, someone will feel the same conviction that moves Me, He probably thought, and they will respond.

This thing about not being accepted, well, it's a common phenomenon in a person's own hometown. Do you remember Lawrence Welk? As a child, Welk knew music was his calling. In his teens, he bought an accordion, but he had to work four years on his father's farm to pay for it. He rented a local opera house and tried to sell concert tickets. Failing to get an audience in his hometown, he decided to go on the road. His father told him he wouldn't last six weeks, but you and I know that his father was wrong. Welk acquired millions of appreciative fans. So, I think the message here is that, when you move to a new stage in life, you can't afford to look back. You have to look ahead. You have to move on. That's what Jesus did.

And you can't afford to have people around you who do not have faith in what you are trying to achieve. In order to succeed, you have to have faith. You have to have belief. And you have to surround yourself with others who believe in you.

Now, there is a potential problem with that word, belief. We have overused that word. It has become so much a part of our "natural" vocabulary that it has lost a lot of its power. But it is still the best word I know. The secret of the way in which Jesus handled the hometown rejection is summed up in that one word, belief: Belief in God, belief in Himself and in others, belief in the future. Jesus was convinced that His task was given by the Father and was inspired by Him. Belief gave Jesus power to survive in the face of the setback. Belief gave Him power to respond in a positive way. And that positive response kept Him in contact with the creative love of God. It kept Him in contact with the love that soared high over the prejudices and narrow judgments of the people of Nazareth. And, because of His belief, He was able to see over what seemed to be a mountain that blocked the road ahead of Him. Although it must have felt like a failure, He was convinced God's plan could not be blocked by the littleness of the faith of Jesus' own people. You and I can make this work for us, too. Believe in yourself. And be sure you have friends surrounding you who believe in you, as well. And of course don't leave God and His plan out.

Dale Carnegie used to tell the story of a man who had once been a good salesman but had fallen on to hard times. Nothing seemed to go right for him anymore. Finally, someone got to know him enough to see his potential. He bought the man a new suit. And immediately his attitude brightened. Within a few days he was on the way back to a successful career. People who believe in you will help you live up to God's desire for you. And they will also help you expand your own self image. And it is no coincidence that Jesus had just selected His twelve closest friends who would continue at His side. That's important, but what's even more important is the ability to see yourself doing what you want to do. If you want to be a great athlete, a famous golfer, an excellent comedian, a doctor, a nurse, a computer expert, a science research specialist, a teacher, a minister, if you want to succeed as a single parent, if you want to recover, or help someone else recover from chemical dependency, whatever you want to do, you have to imagine yourself doing it first.

And you have to realize that it's not all going to be peaches and cream. You have to expect setbacks. You have to expect opposition. You have to expect temptation. That's life. What's the secret? Keep your life steady around belief, belief in God, belief in yourself, and belief in others. That's what will empower you to make whatever adjustments you need to make when you are rejected.

Maybe, sometimes, you don't feel that people treat you with as much respect as you deserve. Maybe at home, or at school or at work, someone else seems to get all the credit that you feel you deserve. It happens. Comedian Rodney Dangerfield made a career out of not getting any respect, from his wife, from his kids, from his parents. He said, "I don't get any respect, not even from my father, he carries around the picture of the kid who came with his wallet instead of me." It happens in families, in communities, in the workplace, in churches, and evidently in the synagogue too. Jesus obviously was in the will of God. But the people in His community would not let Him forget that He was just a carpenter's son.

The interesting thing is that Jesus, even Jesus, could not do any miracles there, *"except to lay His hands on a few sick people and heal them."* He could not do the miracles He had achieved in other places. Even so, that did not slow Him down. He knew who He was. He knew why He was there, to do the will of the Father, and He gave Himself completely to the task at hand. He was determined that He would be all He came to this earth to be. That's a good word for us all. There's a man hanging on a cross who was rejected by His own family, His own town, His own nation. But He saved the world. And He says to us: "Keep the faith. You are a unique creation of the living God. Let no one tell you that you are of little worth. You are of ultimate value to my Father. You are so valuable that I died to save you."

Let me tell you about a young man named Jerry. Jerry had real trouble accepting himself. He didn't get the respect he needed at home. He never fit in with any particular group. He had trouble making friends. His self-esteem was very low. One day in high school, Jerry recalls, he looked in the mirror and realized that he hated himself. He writes: "That day, I made a decision to just exist in this life, to get through it, and to spend the rest of my time dreaming about a place where I would be happy, popular, and influential." Jerry's insecurity and emptiness stayed with him as he entered adulthood. But his whole life changed when he attended a Billy Graham Conference. At the conference, Jerry gained a new image of God, God as a loving Father, as a Creator who intended good for His children. After Jerry gave his life to Jesus, he experienced the kind of love he'd been hearing about. As Jerry grew in his faith, he also learned to like and accept himself. He made friends more easily now, because his self-esteem was firmly rooted in his identity as a child of God.[25] That's where true self respect begins. It's when we realize that we are a child of God. It begins when we realize that Christ died in our behalf. It begins when we hear the Master, who didn't receive any respect from His own people, say to us: "Your sense of identity comes from Me. I respect you. I appreciate you. I died for you. I believe in you. I have a purpose for you. Believe in Me and never question your self-worth again."

What to do when rejected? Believe in Jesus Christ and God's plan for your life through Him. And even if your friends, or your family, or society makes you feel that you are taking one step backwards, by believing in the One who died on the cross for you, just keep on believing, because that is what is needed to take that leap into Life, true Life, abundant Life, and Eternal Life with Christ. Amen.

Not Far from the Kingdom

Mark 12: 28-34

One of the scribes came near and heard them disputing with one another, and seeing that he answered them well, he asked him, "Which commandment is the first of all?" Jesus answered, "The first is, 'Hear, O Israel: the Lord our God, the Lord is one; you shall love the Lord your God with all your heart, and with all your soul, and with all your mind, and with all your strength.' The second is this, 'You shall love your neighbor as yourself.' There is no other commandment greater than these." Then the scribe said to him, "You are right, Teacher; you have truly said that 'he is one, and besides him there is no other'; and 'to love him with all the heart, and with all the understanding, and with all the strength,' and 'to love one's neighbor as oneself,'--this is much more important than all whole burnt offerings and sacrifices." When Jesus saw that he answered wisely, he said to him, "You are not far from the kingdom of God." After that no one dared to ask him any question.

Did you know that we, in the United States, have an estimated 35 million laws on the books? That's a lot more than the ten that we started out with. Now, some of them are very good and deeply needed. But there are others that probably need to be taken off the books. For example: Did you know there is a law in Florida that makes it illegal for a single woman, to parachute out of a plane on Sunday afternoon? Did you know that in Amarillo, Texas, it is against the law to take a bath on Main Street during banking hours? And in Portland, Oregon, it is illegal to wear roller skates in public restrooms? And in St. Louis, there used to be a law that if your, automobile spooked a horse you had to hide the car? And if hiding it didn't work, you had to start dismantling it until the horse calmed down?[26]

Laws are funny. Today in our scripture reading we met a scribe who wanted to talk about Jewish Law, he wanted to know which of the Ten Commandments was the most important. He was a seeker. He wanted to know which one of the commandments would get him closer to God.

Let us pray: May the words of my mouth and the meditations of each of our hearts be acceptable in Your sight, O God, our Rock and our Redeemer. Amen.

In our story today, the scribe seems to know the right answers. Jesus compliments him for this, saying that he is *"not far"* from the Kingdom. But he's still not there yet. Something is missing. His heart seems to be right with God, but he has yet to act on the second half of the command, to love his neighbor as himself. We the church, proclaim that what we cannot ever attain for ourselves, a change of human nature, has been given to us by God. It's a working of God from the inside, which enables us to love our neighbor as ourselves. And this change, wrought by God, is a gift from God. You have probably heard it said: "God loves you just the way you are, but He refuses to leave you that way. He wants you to be just like Jesus."[27] Because of the new identity given to Christians through the Spirit of Christ, we can dare to be different from those around us. Because of the inner workings of God, we can dare to *"love our neighbor as ourselves."* A very important responsibility of church membership is that of being salt and light out in a world gone wild.

You know, the world has its opinion on many things, and many outside the church say that human nature cannot be changed. The world would say that human beings are only capable of thinking of themselves. "Watch out for number one," the world teaches us. But on the contrary, the Christian gospel brings an altogether different point of view. It gives the promise that human nature can be changed, that we can love our neighbor. The Christian gospel teaches us that, because of the indwelling Holy Spirit, we don't have to remain the same.

In short, we all have the opportunity to move closer to God in this life. Take for example, Nicodemus, he was a brilliant member of the Sanhedrin. He was a man, a very wealthy man, who came to Jesus by night. *"Rabbi,"* he said, *"we know that You are a teacher come from God; for no one can do these signs that You do, unless God be with them."[28]* Jesus then shared with Nicodemus the secret, *"You must be born from above."[29]* Nicodemus had come under cover of darkness to avoid prying eyes. He was, after all, a respected leader, a doctor of the Law. Spiritual rebirth had puzzled this intelligent man. It has been puzzling many logical thinkers ever since. I know that personally, because I am probably one of the most logical of the logical thinking people.

You know, birth is a shock; it is radical; and it is also a necessity if a person wishes to live. Likewise, Jesus told Nicodemus that coming to the Kingdom of God was no less radical, and no less essential. He told him that he had to experience the "new birth" a spiritual birth. Did Nicodemus, ever become a useful worker in God's Kingdom? Well we know he defended Jesus against the Pharisees.[30] We also know that he was present after Jesus was crucified.[31] The scriptures don't give us the complete story of his life, but it has always been my hope that the new birth became a reality for him and that he spent the remainder of his life serving the Lord by loving his neighbor.

A couple other good examples of human lives being changed are the Wesley brothers. The year was 1738. John and Charles Wesley were back in England, having experienced a less-than-satisfactory missionary sojourn in the new colony of Georgia. The Wesley brothers were pretty disappointed. Why had Georgia not turned out as the rich and rewarding time they had anticipated it would? After all, both men held a Masters degree from Oxford; they were, both, ordained priests of the Church of England. But, maybe it was because of their logical approach to ministry. Like that of the scribe who viewed everything in life as humanly logical.

John wrote: "All the time I was in Savannah, it was as if I was only beating the air." But, then things began to change. It was Pentecost Sunday, May 21, 1738. Charles was ill. He was staying with a man named, Mr. Bray, at No. 12 in Little Britain. And during that time Bray's sister, Mrs. Turner, was "prompted by a vivid dream" to say something to the young clergyman. She was fearful, but her brother encouraged her, saying: "Speak the words. Christ will do the work." So, she went upstairs and did just that, saying to Charles: "In the name of Jesus of Nazareth, arise, and believe, and you shall be healed of all your infirmities." And he was.[32] Immediately Charles sent for his brother and a group of friends. And he said to them: "I believe." And he told them that he was a new man in Christ. And later, Charles penned these words: O for a thousand tongues to sing my great Redeemer's praise, the glories of my God and King, the triumphs of His grace! My gracious Master and my God, assist me to proclaim, to spread through all the earth abroad the honors of Thy name.

You see, Charles Wesley's heart was finally right with God. He loved God and longed to love his neighbor as himself. And then three days later we hear his brother's account. The day was May 24, 1738 and John carefully recorded the events. At 5 a.m. he read from 2 Peter 1:4: *"There are given unto us... exceeding great and precious promises."* Later that morning he opened his Bible to Mark 12:34, reading: *"Thou art not far from the kingdom of God."* At noon Wesley attended services at St. Paul's where the choir used Henry Purcell's rendition of Psalm 130: *"Out of the deep have I called to thee, O Lord."* The day was fast closing, and Wesley did not want to go to prayer meeting. But he went anyway to the service at Aldersgate Street. In the evening I went, he wrote, very unwillingly to a society in Aldersgate Street, where one was reading Luther's preface to the Epistle to the Romans. About a quarter before nine, while he was describing the change which God works in the heart through faith in Christ, I felt my heart strangely warmed.

I felt I did trust in Christ, Christ alone for salvation; and an assurance was given me that He had taken away my sins, even mine, and saved me from the law of sin and death.[33] John Wesley became a transformed man that day. His heart, like Charles' was finally right with God and his neighbor.

You see, love, according to Jesus is two things: A faithful obedience to God and a gracious desire that God's justice and mercy be extended to our neighbor. In other words, to love God means to say, "Yes!" to God's will with every fiber of your being. And to love neighbor, means being a willing vessel, to allow God to do, through you a portion of His will for the good of your neighbor.

Here are a few examples of what loving our neighbors could look like. There is a tired young mother, in the doctor's waiting room and you offer to watch the toddler while she feeds the baby. There is a person in line at the bank who's stumbling over the English language and struggling to understand deposits and withdrawals and you decide to step out of your line and help him get it straight. Realizing that for the church to be the church, it must reach beyond these four physical walls, you bring your tithes, as well as, your extra mile offerings into God's sanctuary, Sunday after Sunday. There is a neighbor who is struggling to keep his marriage together or there is a college student who is looking for a loving congregation away from home or there is a person in the hospital, whose waiting for someone to pray with them and you take the time out of your busy day to reach out to them in Christian love. With all these acts of kindness, you will move from being *"not far from"* but actually into experiencing God's kingdom for yourself. Don't ever be afraid to do the work that God calls all Christians to. Step out of your comfort zone. Take the risk of being ridiculed. Dare to make mistakes. It's okay. Dare to love God by loving others, even if it means doing something you would not ordinarily do. For, that's exactly what we've been created, redeemed and commanded to do.

That is why we are blessed with this beautiful historical church; that is why we have been blessed with the Alexander House, too, the one we just dedicated to God's service. We have been blessed to be a blessing.

Did you know that there is a wonderful connection between loving your neighbor, and experiencing the kingdom of God? There is. When we love our neighbor as ourselves, not only do they get a glimpse of God's Kingdom, but we ourselves move closer to that Kingdom. *"You are not far from the Kingdom,"* Jesus told the scribe.

Now I suspect that most of us stay in that place of *"not far,"* much more often than not. Our hearts seem to be right with God, but we have yet to take the action needed to love our neighbor as ourselves. And so, like that scribe, we remain *"not far"* from God's Kingdom. But, the good news is, through the power and grace of God, you as a Christian, with God's indwelling Spirit, you can choose to move into experiencing God's Kingdom at any moment. But here is the key. You have to make that choice. You have to choose to yield yourself, your life and all that you have to God. And guess what. There-within lies the mystery of God's transforming and sanctifying power. There-within lies the mystery of how God will fill your heart with the desire to love others. There-within lies the mystery of how God will heal and change you from the inside out. There-within lies the mystery of how God will bless you in this lifetime.

Won't you let Him do His work in you, today? Won't you let God work in you today? Not only, strangely warming your heart, but also, shaping and molding your inner being into what God created you to be? Are you ready to experience what it really means to be a Christian? Are you ready to experience the Kingdom like you've never experienced it before? If so, has God ever got a plan for you!

Let us pray:

Dear heavenly Father, we ask that through the power of Your Holy Spirit You will instill within us, Your people, the desire and ability to truly love You with all of our heart, soul, mind and strength and to also love our neighbor as ourselves. In the name of Jesus, we ask for this sanctifying work within us this day. Amen.

Look Up and Live

Numbers 21:4-9
From Mount Hor they set out by the way to the Red Sea, to go around the land of Edom; but the people became impatient on the way. The people spoke against God and against Moses, "Why have you brought us up out of Egypt to die in the wilderness? For there is no food and no water, and we detest this miserable food." Then the LORD sent poisonous serpents among the people, and they bit the people, so that many Israelites died. The people came to Moses and said, "We have sinned by speaking against the LORD and against you; pray to the LORD to take away the serpents from us." So Moses prayed for the people. And the LORD said to Moses, "Make a poisonous serpent, and set it on a pole; and everyone who is bitten shall look at it and live." So Moses made a serpent of bronze, and put it upon a pole; and whenever a serpent bit someone, that person would look at the serpent of bronze and live.

A volunteer at a nursing home told an interesting story, she said: A 92-year-old widower moved to our nursing home today. And even though he was legally blind, he was a well-poised man, who was fully dressed each morning by eight. After many hours of waiting patiently in the lobby, he smiled sweetly when he was told that his room was ready. As he maneuvered his walker to the elevator, I provided a visual description of his tiny room, including the eyelet sheets that had been hung on his window. I love it, he stated with the enthusiasm of an eight-year-old having just been presented with a new puppy. Mr. Jones, you haven't seen the room; just wait. That doesn't have anything to do with it, he replied. Happiness is something you decide on ahead of time. And I've already decided to love it.

And, he continued saying: Each day is a gift, and as long as my eyes open, I've decided that I'll focus on the new day and all the happy memories I've stored away, just for this time in my life. Now, here was a man who was legally blind, and at the age of 92 could still look up and live each day. He was happy; he was content; it was as if everything was going his way. Why was that, I wonder? That's not the way it was with the people of Israel. No, their attitude was completely the opposite. God had supplied everything that they needed including heavenly food, manna for them to eat in the middle of the desert, but all they could seem to gather into themselves, was an attitude that said: We are not happy.

Now, if we back up a little in the story, we will see that the people of Israel were previously at Mount Sinai where they had received, God's commandments. They spent about a year at that holy mountain. They arrived at Sinai in Exodus 19:1 and they didn't break camp until Numbers 10:11. In our text for today, they are on the move again through the trackless wilderness. And once again Moses hears the familiar lament: *"Why did you bring us out of Egypt to die in this desert, where there is no food or water? We can't stand any more of this miserable food."* Well, this time, the Lord doesn't take kindly to the people's complaining and He sends snakes to punish them. And so, they come to Moses, after a little attitude adjustment and they admit that they have done wrong: *"We have sinned,"* they said, *"We have sinned by speaking against the Lord and against you."*

You know, counselors today tell us that the beginning of healing is to recognize that we do have a problem, healing begins when we decide to take ownership of our own wrongdoings. The people agreed that their mouths had gotten them into this trouble and they pleaded with Moses: *"Please, please, please pray to the LORD to take away the serpents from us."* And so, Moses prays on behalf of the people. He intercedes for them. And it's a good thing too that Moses was there to stand between them and God or else the whole nation might have been destroyed by the poisonous snakes.

His petition for mercy from God was all that the people had. And this wasn't the first time Moses interceded for them, you know. He knew that role well. Obviously, he had been their representative to Pharaoh to get them out of slavery in Egypt. And he was their go-between at Mt Sinai when he received God's Law. And at least one other time, Moses saved the people from certain destruction when God's anger burned against them after worshiping a golden calf. Yes, Moses was definitely a petitioning prophet. When Moses petitioned God, God heard. But He asked Moses to do a strange thing this time. He asked him to make a cast in the form of a snake, fill it with liquid metal and fashion a bronze serpent. Huh?

Then God said something even more, strange! He said: *"Have the people look up at the snake... and they will not die."* Wow! I wonder if Moses hesitated. Why a snake? Well, perhaps because snakes in the ancient world were, not only, a symbol of death and danger, but also, a symbol of life and healing. And we see the snakes on the medical symbol even today. And perhaps the bronze or reddish color would be a foreshadowing of Christ's atonement and purification through blood. But, you know, why not just get rid of the snakes like the people asked Moses to do? That's a good question, I think. Why not just get rid of the snakes? Well, maybe this was God's way of saying that healing will not come until a person recognizes that they have something that is poisoning them, something that they need to be healed of. Now, I'm sure some of the Israelites thought that looking at a bronze snake was stupid. They also died. Others probably remembered the blood on the doorpost to which they looked for salvation many years earlier during the great "Passover," and they believed once again in what Moses was telling them, and they lived.

Today, the prescription is still the same. From the time a snake first tempted Adam and Eve to sin, to the bronze snake in Moses' time, to the time Jesus crushed the serpent's head at Calvary, the medicine is still the same.

What is required is faith in the Son of Man, God in the flesh, being lifted up on the cross. The deadly poison of sin has existed in humankind since the original fall in the Garden. But the perfect sacrifice was lifted up on the cross at Calvary to be Sin for us. Jesus took our place. He's the One who can take the effect of the poison of sin away. And all God asks of us, is that we look up with faith to the Cross of Calvary to see our freedom there.

Some people think it's a foolish thing to trust in the sacrifice of Jesus. The Apostle Paul recognized that, saying: *"For some the cross is foolishness... but for us who are being saved, it is the power of God."[34]* And no, it doesn't make a lot of sense. But it's God's plan of salvation. God came down in the person of Jesus and endured our penalty for us. He crushed the deceiving snake once and for all. You see, God is faithfully consistent. God remains faithful to the agreement that He had made with the people of Israel. And Jesus, Himself, saw the bronze snake story as so significant for our spiritual life that He applied if to Himself. The snake on a tree foreshadowed the nailing of Jesus to the cross. Jesus said: *"Just as Moses lifted up the serpent in the wilderness, so must the Son of Man be lifted up."[35]*

For the children of Israel, the wilderness was that time between God's deliverance from Egypt and their entry into the Promised Land. In our life, the wilderness is that time between now and when Christ returns. Right now though, we are on our wilderness journey. We live in the in-between-time. And in our wilderness journey, we too have "snakes" that we have to contend with, snakes that poison our lives. Yes, we like the Israelites, are living in our wilderness, only the geography is different. And in that place God says to us: Look up and live. He says: Look up to the Cross and see there the sign of your healing, the sign of your salvation.

Our God knows that living can be hard in this life and that our suffering can be great. Our God, in Christ, has experienced that wilderness living Himself. And so, He provides a solution, a Cross that proclaims to us that His love and acceptance and forgiveness is not based upon: Our Successes, or our Ability to always make good choices, or our Social standing, or our Bank accounts, or our Prestige, or our Grade averages in school, or our I.Q. No, God's great and unconditional love is not based on any of that. God sent Jesus for "all" people, and gives Eternal Life to those who choose to receive Him. Look up and Live, He says. See there your Redeemer and know *"that whoever believes in Him shall not perish, but shall have eternal life."* The time has arrived, I think, for the church to get its focus back on the Cross, to look up and to live. What a witness that would be, if the whole church were to Look up to the Cross of Christ.

Remember the 92 year old man who said: "Each day is a gift." Well, he also suggested five ways a person can live to the age of 92 and still be happy. These are the five things he suggested: Free your heart from hatred; free your mind from worries; live simply; give more; expect less. Now when I first read those things, I thought, well with age comes wisdom, but then I realized that everything listed there, was biblical and they reflect Jesus' own words. Free your heart from hatred – *"Love your enemies"* (Luke 6:27). Free your mind from worries – *"Do not worry about your life"* (Matthew 6:25). Live simply – *"Look at the birds of the air how simple they are... yet God provides for them"* (Matthew 6:26). Give more – *"Give, and it will be given to you. A good measure, pressed down, shaken together and running over"* (Luke 6:38). Expect less – *"And when you love... expect nothing in return for your reward will be great in heaven"* (Luke 6:35).

In other words, look up to Jesus Christ and live. Allow His love to flow through you. Depend upon God's good provisions. Don't store up for yourself, too many of the material things of this life. But share unselfishly what's given to you. And finally, don't expect so much from other people, but learn that the only One who can bring true happiness and contentment is God, Himself.

During the time of Israel's wandering, the prescription was given: "Look up and Live," and they did. And amazingly, the grumbling finally stopped and they became content. You see, our story today included the last recorded complaint of the wandering Israelites. Isn't that interesting? Perhaps they finally learned what they needed to know about God and His ways during that time. Perhaps we can learn the same in our wilderness journey. Perhaps we, too, can finally become content in God's provision in Christ, as we Look up to Him and Live. Amen.

When I Am Lifted Up

John 12:20-33

Now among those who went up to worship at the festival were some Greeks. They came to Philip, who was from Bethsaida in Galilee, and said to him, "Sir, we wish to see Jesus." Philip went and told Andrew; then Andrew and Philip went and told Jesus. Jesus answered them, "The hour has come for the Son of Man to be glorified. Very truly, I tell you, unless a grain of wheat falls into the earth and dies, it remains just a single grain; but if it dies, it bears much fruit. Those who love their life lose it, and those who hate their life in this world will keep it for eternal life. Whoever serves me must follow me, and where I am, there will my servant be also. Whoever serves me, the Father will honor. "Now my soul is troubled. And what should I say--'Father, save me from this hour'? No, it is for this reason that I have come to this hour. Father, glorify your name." Then a voice came from heaven, "I have glorified it, and I will glorify it again." The crowd standing there heard it and said that it was thunder. Others said, "An angel has spoken to him." Jesus answered, "This voice has come for your sake, not for mine. Now is the judgment of this world; now the ruler of this world will be driven out. And I, when I am lifted up from the earth, will draw all people to myself." He said this to indicate the kind of death he was to die.

The world today prefers to be neutral. It does not want to offend anyone. It does not like having to decide. In the world that is called tolerance, but in eternity it will be called despair.

Let us pray: May the words of my mouth and the meditations of each of our hearts be acceptable in Your sight, O God, our Rock and our Redeemer. Amen.

It was judgment time. And "the Judge," God Himself was about to take upon Himself what the world deserved. Jesus' death on the cross would pay the price for sin and save those who turned to Him.[36] In the crowd that day, pressing in to see Jesus, were some Greeks, some proselytes, Jewish converts, who were at the Feast of the Passover. And they sought to see Jesus through one of His disciples, who had a Greek name, Philip. Now, we have no idea of what they really expected to see or hear from Jesus. But, they must have been shocked when He used the occasion to make a most serious announcement, saying: *The hour has come for the Son of Man to be glorified... Those who love their life will lose it, and those who hate their life in this world will keep it for eternal life.*[37] Jesus was headed for the cross. He was to be "lifted up" on the cross. It was a moment He had been preparing for. The time had come. It was necessary. It could not be avoided. He used the analogy of the grain of wheat that must die in the earth and then He added: *And I, when I am lifted up from the earth, I will draw all people to Myself.*[38] His being lifted up, of course, was His description of the Cross, but for John, the writer of the fourth Gospel, it also included the Resurrection and later Jesus' Ascension into heaven.

But, you see, Jesus this day draws a line in the sand saying, the time for debating is over. Those who would be My disciples must lose their life in order to save it for eternity. But, some Greeks of the Jewish faith were still debating about Rabbi Jesus that day, and debates still go on, even today.

For example: The Islam religion says that, Jesus is the son of Mary.[39] It is true that the Qur'an itself affirms that Jesus was born of Mary. But there ends the similarities between the Islam religion and the Christian faith. Have you read the teachings of Islam or, the Qur'an? Interesting books, but they don't portray Christian beliefs accurately.

Let me just share a little bit with you. Going against the New Testament witness, Muslim's are taught that Jesus did not die.[40] While Christians believe that Jesus ascended into heaven after He was crucified, Muslims are taught that Jesus ascended, so as to be saved from the cross, before He was crucified. Why? Well, because, in the Islamic teaching, atonement and forgiveness of sin through Jesus' death on a cross would be unthinkable. Muslims are taught that Jesus asked Allah to save Him from the cross and that His ascent to heaven was Allah's answer to that prayer. But in our scripture reading today we hear Jesus Himself saying: *My soul is troubled. And what should I say – Father, save Me from this hour? No, it is for this reason that I have come to this hour.*[41] You see, according to Islamic teaching, Jesus was only a prophet of Allah, who performed miracles only by Allah's leave. And the Crucifixion, well according to Islam, it was merely a Christian myth.

The Qur'an also teaches that the Christian doctrine of the Trinity consists of God, Jesus and Mary, not the Holy Spirit. Mary is divine in their inaccurate teaching.[42] And the Holy Spirit is left out all together. Anyone who reads the Qur'an can see that the Spirit of Christ is obviously missing in its teachings on Christian beliefs, because Muslims and their leader know nothing of that Spirit, the One who was sent, from the Father, and promised by the Son, on the Day of Pentecost, the Birthday of the Church.

And here is a most disturbing statement, found in the Sahih Muslim hadith, Book #25, a compilation of quotes from Allah's prophet. Muhammad's scribe wrote down and his followers preserved these revealing words. Muhammad said: The most wretched person in the sight of Allah on the Day of Resurrection and the worst person and Target of Allah's wrath would be al-Amlaak (the one Christians call the King of kings) for there is no king but Allah.[43] You see, in the end it is not the God we know, it is not the Person Jesus called Father, who the followers of Muhammad are taught to revere in any sense of the word.

In fact, according to the Muslim bible that is "blasphemy,"[44] because, Allah has no son."[45] Even so, we must give all those who inquire of Jesus some credit. And we need to remember that it is not the Muslim who is bad or evil, but instead it is what they have been taught; it is the foundational teachings of their leader who was not Holy Spirit led. And some, at this point in the conversation, would argue that they know a good Muslim who doesn't follow the foundational teachings of their religion. Well, then I think that John Wesley and I would say that, that person is an "Almost Muslim." But, here's what it boils down to. God created each one of us, even the Muslim and the "Almost Muslim." God loves each one of us, and God weeps for all who do not know of His love for them. Jesus said: *"Love those who are against you and pray for those who persecute you."*[46] So, our calling, our calling as the Church is to love and pray for those who do not know of God's love for them, we are called to love everyone with a Christ-like love. And then, leave the rest to God.

Jesus also said: *"I am sending you out like sheep into the midst of wolves; so be wise as serpents and innocent as doves."*[47] It is important that the church educate itself, concerning the teachings of other religions, and then, and then respond in grace and love, as Christ has responded to us, even when we were yet sinners.

Next, Hinduism; Hinduism is the religion of multiple gods. Their land is peppered with more than 300,000 local deities. But concerning Jesus and as their folk-story goes, as a teenager, He slipped away from home, journeyed across South East Asia to learn yoga meditation, and then returned to Israel to become a guru to the Jews. Now, some Hindus, like Gandhi, are drawn to Jesus because of His compassion and nonviolence, but they don't really revere Him as we would think of reverence. Jesus is nothing more to them than, a guru – a guide to self realization. Hinduism, says all of human beings, including Jesus, have the potential to discover their own inherent divinity, whether you call it: A god-consciousness, a Krishna-consciousness, or a Buddha consciousness.

And how could they say anything different? After all, theirs is a religion of over 300,000 deities. It's all the same to them; one god is as good as the next. And, they take this "inherent divinity" idea to its natural conclusion, saying: If we are all inherently divine then we are all in essence one-and-the-same being. We will get to that just in a minute. But first let's go from a religion of over 300,000 deities to a religion that seems to have no deity at all, Buddhism.

Buddhism is interesting because the life stories of Jesus and the Buddha are strikingly similar. It is reported in some traditions that Buddha was conceived by a virgin just as Jesus. Both leave home for the wilderness where each is tempted by a Satan figure. Both return enlightened, work miracles and challenge the religious establishment by their teachings. Both attract disciples and both are betrayed by one of them. Both preach compassion, unselfishness and giving to others and each creates a movement that bears the founder's name. Some might say that Jesus found His model in Buddha, except for the fact that the man who started the Buddhist movement, Gautama Buddha, lived 600 years after Jesus. He was born into a noble family on the borders of India and Nepal, grew up as a Hindu, the faith of 300,000 deities, and then rejected certain tenants of that faith. Buddha's teachings can be summed up in four points, called the Four Noble Truths: Sorrow is the universal human experience. The cause of sorrow is desire. Sorrow can be eliminated by removing desire. Desire, this unwanted emotion, can be systematically abandoned by doing certain things by following Buddha's Noble 8-fold path of removal. And, if a person can get rid of that desire, Buddha says, then they can pass from this world of "individual existence" into the world of pure Being, Nirvana. It is the goal of every Buddhist to achieve Buddha-hood, to become Buddha himself, to achieve Nirvana.

But, as Randy Alcorn states in his book on Heaven: "Christians must distinguish the biblical promises, from the beliefs of Buddhism, Hinduism, or New Age mysticism, in which individuality is, assimilated into Nirvana. Though God will be absorbing, we will not be absorbed by Him. Though we may feel lost in God's vastness, we will not lose our identity, instead we will find it."[48] As scripture teaches us, whoever loses his or her life will find it, eternally, through a promised resurrected body.

And finally, there's Judaism. Among Jewish people today, most would agree that Jesus was Himself, a Jew. That much is agreed upon. But that is about all the similarities there are when we compare Jewish and Christian beliefs, about Jesus. Today, in Jewish circles, Jesus is almost completely ignored among most of the people, except for a group of Jewish students and scholars, who are trying to understand Him better. Rabbi Neusner, who wrote a book entitled <u>A Rabbi Talks With Jesus</u>, imagines himself, as meeting up with Jesus and he writes: I can see myself meeting this man, and with courtesy, arguing with Him. And I can see myself, challenging Him on the bases of our shared Torah, the first five books of the Old Testament. I can also imagine myself saying: Friend, you go your way, I'll go mine, I wish you well – without me. Yours is not the Torah of Moses that I know, and all I have from God, and all I will ever need from God is the Torah of Moses. And then he concludes: He would have gone His way to glory, I my way to my duties and my responsibilities.

Well, a Christian might say: You are correct, Rabbi. The Torah teaches that we must sanctify life in the here and now of home and family, community and society. But that same Torah, the one you hold dear, told Abraham to sacrifice his own son. It was a test of Abraham's faith, but the threat to that young boy's life was real. And it was God who provided the sacrifice, at the last moment. And in that story we have the life of Jesus of Nazareth, foretold. The God of Jesus and the God of that young boy, Isaac, are one in the same God. But the difference, during the life of Jesus, is that God did not stop the second sacrifice.

Why? Well, because it wasn't some young innocent boy being led to the slaughter, it was God Himself, God in the flesh, Rabbi, who gave His life willingly, so that no one else would have to be sacrificed because of their own sinfulness.

Here-in lies the difference. Here is what the Greeks did not see. Here is what the disciples could not perceive. Here is what the Rabbi could not accept: The Cross, the lifting up of Jesus on the cross, is what separates the Christ of Christianity from every other Jesus. In Islam, the story of Jesus' death is rejected as an insult to their god, Allah. And Hindus can accept only a Jesus who passes into a peaceful state of self realization. And for Buddhists, the figure of a crucified Christ "Doesn't contain joy or peace or do justice to Jesus," their inferior Buddha.[49] And the Jews, argue that there is no model for a crucified Messiah in the Old Testament Scriptures. You see, there is no room in other religions for the Cross, for the lifting up of Christ, for the offer of salvation to a fallen humanity.

Have you heard the statement: "What you see is what you get?" Now, it is true that what a person ultimately sees is dependent upon their angle of vision. And, a persons' view of the cross depends largely upon their view of who they believe Jesus really is. You know, I wonder what those Greeks finally decided about Jesus that day, when He responded to them, saying: *The hour has come for the Son of Man to be glorified... and I, when I am lifted up from the earth, will draw all people to Myself.*[50] I wonder which Jesus they saw. I wonder if there was room in their view for a crucified and Risen Christ. Which Jesus do you see? Is there room in your view for a crucified and Risen Christ? Is there a need in your heart for a Savior?

That is a most pertinent question. Is there room in your heart, for the "Christ of Christianity?" Is there room in your view for a crucified and Risen Christ? That's the question for all, who inquire about Jesus, even today. Amen.

What's New?

Jeremiah 31:31-34
The days are surely coming, says the LORD, when I will make a new covenant with the house of Israel and the house of Judah. It will not be like the covenant that I made with their ancestors when I took them by the hand to bring them out of the land of Egypt--a covenant that they broke, though I was their husband, says the LORD. But this is the covenant that I will make with the house of Israel after those days, says the LORD: I will put my law within them, and I will write it on their hearts; and I will be their God, and they shall be my people. No longer shall they teach one another, or say to each other, "Know the LORD," for they shall all know me, from the least of them to the greatest, says the LORD; for I will forgive their iniquity, and remember their sin no more.

What's new? is a common greeting. And there are many answers people give: A new car, a new house, a new boat, a new suit, a new dress, a new coat. Others focus more on relationships than material things answering: A new boyfriend or girlfriend, a new husband or wife or a new acquaintance. But Jeremiah, the prophet, focuses not so much on things of the earth or on human relationship but instead, he focuses on a personal relationship with an Eternal God. He writes: *The days are surely coming, says the Lord, when I will make a new covenant with the house of Israel and the house of Judah.*[51] Notice that the prophet says: *"The days are coming."* In other words, something New is out there in the future. Something New and fresh is to be anticipated. The time had arrived when a vision was needed to project something New. And Jeremiah had that vision. Jeremiah saw that the people had broken the covenant that God had established with them when He brought them out of Egypt.

Jeremiah saw that they had gone the broad way that leads to destruction instead of the narrow way that God had shown them. But, he also saw beyond what he could see with his eyes. Jeremiah saw a New Day and a New Way.

Let us pray: May the words of my mouth and the meditations of each of our hearts be acceptable in Your sight, O God, our Rock and our Redeemer. Amen.

Jeremiah saw that something New was coming. So, he searched his mind for a way to describe the overwhelming change that he foresaw, and then he called it *"a New Covenant."*[52] And this New Covenant gave hope to a people who were down and out during Jeremiah's time. And it also looked forward to a time when God's Law would be written on the hearts of God's people.[53] In other words, this New Covenant with God would be inward, not just outward, the Prophet said. This New Covenant would be centered on obeying God out of love, instead of fear. This New Covenant would be all about an intimate relationship with God, Himself. The people would know God.[54] They would know God personally. *"Something new is coming,"* Jeremiah says. The time is coming when people who have forgotten to remember God will remember Him once more.

Another prophet, Isaiah, also spoke of a New personal relationship with God, through a Suffering Servant.[55] We pick up the story of the Savior of the New Covenant in Isaiah. The Savior of the New Covenant was oppressed and afflicted, like a lamb that is led to the slaughter (Isaiah 53:7). A perversion of justice caused His death (Isaiah 53:8a). He was stricken for our transgression (Isaiah 53:8b). All of this suffering crushed Him, yet it was part of God's plan (Isaiah 53:10a), because God Himself, would become an offering for the peoples sin (Isaiah 53:10b). Jesus, the Suffering Servant of Isaiah, died on the cross to save people from their sin. The New Covenant that was promised by Jeremiah was fulfilled through Jesus Christ, God, Himself, as His plan was carried out.

At the Last Supper, Jesus said: *"Take, eat; this is my body."* Then *He took a cup, and after giving thanks He gave it to them saying, "Drink of it all of you; for this is my blood of the New covenant which is poured out for many for the forgiveness of sins."*[56] Something New is in the Lord's Supper.

And the Gospel of John refers to that Newness as "Light." *In him Jesus, the Word was life and the life was the light of all people.*[57] That Light came, shone brightly, but not all believed what they saw. The Light shone in the darkness, but some people were spiritually blind and did not comprehend the Light, but neither did they overcome the Light.[58] Jesus, the Light, is New. John 12:20-33 tells us that people of all cultures and races seek the Light in Jesus. *"Sir, we wish to see Jesus,"* the Greeks told Philip. And when Philip told Jesus about the people who wanted to see Him, Jesus said: *"When I am lifted up from the earth, I will draw all peoples to Myself."*[59] That's something New. That's the New Covenant in action. But there is even more to this Newness. Hear the vision in Revelation when the One seated on the throne says: *"See, I am making all things new."*[60] In Revelation, Jesus, the Suffering Servant of Isaiah, speaks of the day when all things will be made New, He speaks of the last day, when there will be a New Earth and a New Heaven.

Here's a story about Heaven. I think you will like it. It seems that two sisters in their nineties died at the same time and went to Heaven. There they were overwhelmed by the magnificence and glory of heaven. They ooh-ed and ah-ed at the wonders they saw. They couldn't get over what a matchless place it was. Then one said to the other, "You know, we could have been here five years earlier if you hadn't insisted on our eating oat bran." Ah, yes, Heaven is going to be great. How do we know that? Well, scripture tells us that. John, the writer of Revelation, in lonely exile on the little Mediterranean island of Patmos was given a vision of Heaven and there we find wonders beyond description.

Four times the word, "New," is used to describe Heaven: *"a New heaven," "a New earth," "New Jerusalem,"* and Jesus' words: *"Behold, I make all things New."* The word "New" is heavily emphasized because life in Heaven will be different from life on earth as we know it today. It will be renewed, redeemed. In Isaiah we hear that: *"The former things have passed away."*[61] But, in Matthew we hear Jesus saying: *At the renewal of all things... you who have followed Me will also sit on twelve thrones.*[62] It is also in Matthew that we hear: *"Blessed are the meek, for they will inherit the earth."*[63] You see, in Heaven we will be endlessly surprised at what our inheritance will include.

John Alcorn writes a whole book on Heaven and in his introduction he says: By the time you finish reading this book, you will have a biblical basis for envisioning the eternal Heaven. You will understand that in order to get a picture of Heaven – which will one day be centered on the New Earth – you don't need to look up at the clouds; you simply need to look around you and imagine what all this would be like without sin and death and suffering and corruption. Then he adds an illustration, saying: As I anticipated my first glimpse of Heaven, I remembered the first time I went snorkeling. I saw countless fish of every shape, size, and color. And just when I thought I'd seen the most beautiful fish, along came another even more striking. Etched in my memory is a certain sound – the sound of a gasp going through my rubber snorkel as my eyes were opened to that breathtaking underwater world. I imagine our first glimpse of Heaven will cause us to similarly gasp in amazement and delight. The first gasp will likely be followed by many more as we continually encounter new sights in that endlessly wonderful place. And that will be just the beginning because we will not see our real eternal home – the New Earth – until the resurrection of the dead. And it will be far better than anything we've ever seen before. So look out a window. Take a walk. Talk with your friend. Use your God-given skill to paint or draw or build a shed or write a book. But imagine it – all of it – in its original condition.

Think of friends or family members who loved Jesus and are with Him now. Picture them with you, walking together in this place. All of you have powerful bodies, stronger than those of an Olympic decathlete. You are laughing, playing, talking, and reminiscing. Now you see someone coming toward you. It's Jesus, with a big smile on his face. You fall to your knees in worship. He pulls you up and embraces you. At last, you're with the person you were made for, in the place you were made to be. Everywhere you go there will be new people and places to enjoy, new things to discover. What's that you smell? A feast! A party's ahead. And you're invited. There's exploration and work to be done – and you can't wait to get started.[64] One thing Heaven will never be: It will not be a let-down. The Good News proclaimed on earth will become the Fantastic News displayed in Heaven.

John wrote in the Book of Revelation: *Then I saw a new heaven and a new earth; for the first heaven and the first earth had passed away. And I saw the holy city, the new Jerusalem, coming down out of heaven from God, prepared as a bride adorned for her husband.*[65] Central among all the glories of Heaven will be the majesty of God who is seated on the throne. He is the heart of Heaven. It was not just a voice, but a loud voice that came from Heaven's throne, saying: *Look, here God lives among human beings. He will make his home among them; they will be his people, and he will be their God, God-with-them.*[66]

But, if there is a New Heaven and a New Earth, what will happen to the old one? Will the present Earth be utterly destroyed? No, I don't think so. Second Peter 3:10 states: *The day of the Lord will come... the heavens will pass away... and the earth and everything that is done on it will be disclosed.* And 1 Corinthians states: *If anyone builds on the foundation with gold, silver, precious stones, wood, hay, straw – the work of each builder will become visible, for the Day will disclose it, because it will be revealed with fire, and the fire will test what sort of work each has done. But if what has been built on the foundation survives, the builder will receive a reward.*[67]

The key to understanding the meaning of this image of destruction lies within the passages themselves. In 2 Peter we hear that "everything that has been done on earth will be disclosed" and in 1 Corinthians Paul writes: But, some things will "survive." So, if everything will be disclosed and some things will survive, then it stands to reason that there will not be total destruction. Think about the destruction of the earth during the Great Flood in Noah's time. The flood was certainly cataclysmic and devastating. But did it obliterate the world, making it cease to exist? No, Noah and his family and the animals were delivered from God's judgment in order to re-inhabit a cleansed world made ready for them by God. But even with that said, the destruction by fire will be even more powerful. Because, the cleansing with fire will also permanently, eliminate sin; everything will be disclosed. What is good and glorifies God will survive, what is not good will be burned up. Scripture points to the fact that in the end, the earth will not be lost; it will not be utterly destroyed. Instead, it will be Redeemed, Resurrected, and Restored to its original wholeness. God will bring about a New Earth.

And here's the best part. All of the things of the old Earth that matter: *Whatever is true, whatever is honorable, whatever is just, whatever is pure, whatever is pleasing, whatever is commendable, whatever is excellent or worthy of praise,*[68] all those things will be drawn into, the New Earth. If it glorified God on this present earth, it will glorify God on the New Earth. The New Earth will be a place of healing.[69] Christ's healing ministry was just a foretaste, a glimpse of Heaven, the place where all hurts are healed, all suffering forever eclipsed by joy. As Alcorn states: We won't overeat or under eat on the New Earth. With health, vitality, and freedom, we'll all get plenty of activity. We certainly won't experience heart disease, diabetes, asthma, osteoporosis, arthritis, cancer, MS, HIV or anything else that consumes the body. No matter what we look like, our bodies will please the Lord, ourselves, and others. We won't gaze into the mirror wishing for a different nose or different cheeks, ears, or teeth.

The sinless beauty of the inner person will overflow into the beauty of the outer person. We'll feel neither insecurity nor arrogance. We won't attempt to hide or impress. We won't have to *try* to look beautiful – we *will* be beautiful.[70] So here's the bottom line, this New Earth, it will cater to the wholeness and health (body, mind and spirit) of all who reside there, to all who humbled themselves in this lifetime, to all who accepted God's plan of Salvation in this lifetime. To them, this New Heaven and New Earth will be eternally accessible.

So, what New things do we have to look forward to? Everything, a New Heaven, a New Earth, a New body. Everything will be Renewed and Redeemed, with an Eternal Redemption, for those who choose the "Narrow Way," God's Plan of Salvation. So be it. Amen.

The Word Became Flesh

John 1:1-14
In the beginning was the Word, and the Word was with God, and the Word was God. He was in the beginning with God. All things came into being through him, and without him not one thing came into being. What has come into being in him was life, and the life was the light of all people. The light shines in the darkness, and the darkness did not overcome it. There was a man sent from God, whose name was John. He came as a witness to testify to the light, so that all might believe through him. He himself was not the light, but he came to testify to the light. The true light, which enlightens everyone, was coming into the world. He was in the world, and the world came into being through him; yet the world did not know him. He came to what was his own, and his own people did not accept him. But to all who received him, who believed in his name, he gave power to become children of God, who were born, not of blood or of the will of the flesh or of the will of man, but of God. And the Word became flesh and lived among us, and we have seen his glory, the glory as of a father's only son, full of grace and truth.

Today's message is going to have a Christmas theme. You know, I figure that if the stores can start with all the Christmas sales, then we can talk about Christmas in October. Makes sense to me. There was once a Christmas pageant presented by a class of 4-year-olds, and it was an evening to remember. It began with the 3 virgin Marys marching out onto the stage. Now, it's not every Christmas pageant that has 3 virgin Marys, but over the years the school had acquired 3 Mary costumes, and so, quite naturally the script was revised. This gave a chance for more children to be involved and kept down the arguing over who got the leading roles.

The 2 Josephs walked up behind the Marys. Then 23 little angels came out. They were dressed in white robes and huge gauze wings. They were followed by 20 little shepherd boys, dressed in burlap sacks and carrying shepherds crooks. It was at this point that the problem occurred. During the rehearsal the teacher had used chalk to draw circles on the floor to mark where the angels were supposed to stand and crosses to mark the spots of the shepherds. But the children had practiced with their regular clothes on. So, on the night of the pageant, when the angels came walking out and stood on their circles, their very large, but beautiful, gauze wings covered the crosses of the shepherds. So when the time came for the shepherds to find their places, they did not know where to stand. There was one little boy who became extremely frustrated and angry over the whole experience. He finally spied his teacher behind the curtains and shocked everyone when he said in a loud stage whisper: "Because of these angels, I can't find the cross."[71] I wonder if that can't happen sometimes. The romantic elements of Christmas, the shepherds, the wise men, the angels, the star in the East, not to mention the commercialism of Christmas, have a tendency to obscure the true meaning of the birth of Christ, a birth that leads to a cross, that leads to salvation.

Let us pray: May the words of my mouth and the meditations of each of our hearts be acceptable in Your sight, O God, our Rock and our Redeemer. Amen.

In John's prologue, there are no angels, no shepherds, no star, not even Mary and Joseph. Instead there is some of the most beautiful and important theological language to be found. John writes: *In the beginning was the Word, and the Word was with God, and the Word was God. He was in the beginning with God. All things came into being through Him, and without Him not one thing came into being. What has come into being in Him was life, and the life was the light of all people. The light shines in the darkness, and the darkness did not overcome it. The true light, which enlightens everyone, was coming into the world.*

And the Word became flesh and lived among us, and we have seen His glory, the glory as of a father's only son, full of grace and truth.[72] No shepherds, no angels, no star, yet here, ultimately is the story of Christmas.

Max Lucado in his book, <u>God Came Near</u>, descriptively writes about the Word becoming flesh. He says: The omnipotent, in one instant, made Himself breakable. He who had been spirit became pierceable. He who was larger than the universe had become an embryo. God as a fetus. Holiness sleeping in a womb.[73] God took on human form. Now, for many, this is an uncomfortable thing to accept. It is easier to keep God at a distance, some feel. But Lucado goes on to say something quite different. He continues: Let God be as human as He intended to be. Let Him into the mire and muck of our world. For only if we let Him in can He pull us out.[74] And that's exactly what God did for us.

Listen to this story. You'll probably recognize the person, right off. He's a man who let God into the "mire and muck" of his life. His name is George Foreman. He made sports history when at the age of 45 he won the Heavyweight Boxing Championship of the World. However, unknown to most was the reason he fought and to whom he credited the victory. About his youth, George said: "I was a mean, ugly, cantankerous, horrible person, but then Jesus Christ came into my life as Lord and Savior." That one event changed George from an arrogant man to an ambassador for Christ. Foreman has spent the last part of his life preaching and sharing the gospel with people on the streets in Houston, Texas. He built a church with his own money. He built a Youth Center to keep young people off the streets, and off drugs, and out of bars and clubs. And then, he needed money to support the work he had started. So he used the skills he had. He went back into the ring. Foreman though, says the real victory is in what Christ has done for him. He says he can't comprehend why he would have been so bad in the past.

Friends and family today call him a gracious, articulate, sensitive man and his daughter, Natalie at age 14, said: "The most important thing in his life is praising God." Now, the thing for us to see here is that the same victory can be ours if we allow God to enter deeply into our struggles.

John the evangelist writes: *"The people who walked in darkness have seen a great light."* God sets up residence right smack dab in the middle of the darkness. The scriptures tell us that 2000 years ago in Bethlehem, a baby changed the atmosphere for all who came to know Him. But, so much religion these days seems powerless to change anybody anymore. Why is that? Well, because we have reduced it to the discussion of an idea, or the trust in a physical book. What you need, if your life has become troubled or empty, is a Word that has become flesh, an idea that took on physical form, an embodied event, a personal relationship with the Word that became flesh and walked this earth.

God could have said: "Here's an idea that will save the world if you only believe it." But that is not how God has come among us. He didn't come among us as an idea. God has said: "Here is a person. Not only do I want you to trust in Him, His life, His death and His resurrection, but I also want you to follow Him, to take that Light into your heart and then to shine it back out into a dark world. God could have said: "Here is a sacred document. Accept whatever it says." But God did not come among us as a book, but instead as flesh and blood, born in the city of David, in the days of Herod, the King.

John's Gospel brings home to us the fact that the Christmas story is not about an act of humanity, but about an act of God, a deliberate act of God. When we could do nothing for ourselves, God stepped in to save us.

Paul Harvey gives us a picture of God's salvation as it takes place in one man's heart. You've probably heard the story; it is one of my favorites. Harvey writes: The man to whom I'm going to introduce you was not a scrooge; he was a kind, decent, mostly good man, generous to his family, upright in his dealings with other men. But he just didn't believe all that incarnation stuff which the churches proclaim at Christmas time. It just didn't make sense and he was too honest to pretend otherwise. He just couldn't swallow the Jesus Story, about God coming to Earth as a man. "I'm truly sorry to distress you," he told his wife, "but I'm not going with you to church this Christmas Eve." He said he'd feel like a hypocrite and that he'd much rather just stay at home, but that he would wait up for them. And so he stayed and they went to the midnight service.

Shortly after the family drove away in the car, snow began to fall. He went to the window to watch the flurries getting heavier and heavier and then went back to his fireside chair and began to read his newspaper. Minutes later he was startled by a thudding sound, then another, and then another, sort of a thump or a thud. At first he thought someone must be throwing snowballs against his living room window. But when he went to the front door to investigate he found a flock of birds huddled miserably in the snow. They'd been caught in the storm and, in a desperate search for shelter, had tried to fly through his large landscape window. Well, he couldn't let the poor creatures lie there and freeze, so he remembered the barn where his children stabled their pony. That would provide a warm shelter, if he could direct the birds to it. Quickly he put on a coat and galoshes, and tramped through the deepening snow to the barn. He opened the doors wide and turned on a light, but the birds did not come in. He figured food would entice them in. So he hurried back to the house, got bread crumbs and sprinkled them on the snow, making a trail to the yellow-lighted wide open doorway of the stable. But to his dismay, the birds ignored the bread crumbs, and continued to flap around helplessly in the snow.

He tried catching them. He tried shooing them into the barn by walking around them waving his arms. Instead, they scattered in every direction, except into the warm, lighted barn. And then, he realized that they were afraid of him. To them, he reasoned, I am a strange and terrifying creature. If only I could think of some way, to let them know that they can trust me that I am not trying to hurt them, but to help them. But how? Because, any move he made tended to frighten them, confuse them. They just would not follow. They would not be led or shooed because they feared him. "If only I could be a bird," he thought to himself, "and mingle with them and speak their language. Then I could tell them to not be afraid. Then I could show them the way to the safe, warm, to the safe warm barn. But I would have to be one of them so they could see, and hear and understand."

At that moment the church bells began to ring. The sound reached his ears above the sounds of the wind. And he stood there listening to the bells - listening to the bells ringing out the glad tidings of Christmas. And he sank to his knees in the snow.[75] The Gospel of John tells us that Jesus Christ is, Life, and the Light, for all people. It tells us that God revealed Himself to us in the only way He could without overwhelming us. God became a tiny babe. He was born into this world. John recorded that fact, saying: *God came to that which was His own.* God became flesh. And because of that, we don't need to fear anything any longer.

This manger child, this Word that walked around, has remade millions-upon-millions of lives. He can remake your life, too. You can be born again. You can be free from fear and anxiety and despair. You can have His Spirit in your heart. You don't need to search any further for the true meaning and purpose of life. You don't need to be subject to the powers of this world that can tear your life apart. You can be Whole, Saved, Redeemed. That's the good news of our Lord, Jesus Christ. That's the good news of Christmas, even in October. Amen.

True Wisdom

James 3:13-18; 4:7-8a
Who is wise and understanding among you? Show by your good life that your works are done with gentleness born of wisdom. But if you have bitter envy and selfish ambition in your hearts, do not be boastful and false to the truth. Such wisdom does not come down from above, but is earthly, unspiritual, devilish. For where there is envy and selfish ambition, there will also be disorder and wickedness of every kind. But the wisdom from above is first pure, then peaceable, gentle, willing to yield, full of mercy and good fruits, without a trace of partiality or hypocrisy. And a harvest of righteousness is sown in peace for those who make peace. Submit yourselves therefore to God. Resist the devil, and he will flee from you. Draw near to God, and he will draw near to you.

Do you remember back in 1984 when the federal government decided to sponsor the building of an atomic particle accelerator in Texas? Planners said the enormous and astronomically expensive atom smasher would dwarf any other in the world. It would take us several steps closer, they said, to discovering the secrets of the universe. The particle accelerator was to be built underground, and so with the blessing of government money, construction began on a circular tunnel, which, if it had been completed, would have been several miles in circumference. But then congress had second thoughts about the cost of the particle accelerator and construction came to a halt. What is now left after the workers have abandoned the job site is a five-mile, slightly curved tunnel large enough to accommodate a truck. And the problem, well the tunnel goes nowhere. And now the question arises: Does this tunnel that goes nowhere have any use?

Well, someone thinks so. The tunnel contains the ideal conditions, a businessman says, for growing mushrooms.[76] Now think about that. A multi-multi-multi-million dollar tunnel built to discover the secrets of the universe, being used as a mushroom farm. You know, James was right; there is a definite difference between human knowledge and godly wisdom. And unless we seek to know God, all of our seemingly sophisticated knowledge will go nowhere. We will wind up with mushrooms, rather than the marvelous mind of God.

Let us pray: May the words of my mouth and the meditations of each of our hearts be acceptable in Your sight, O God, our Rock and our Redeemer. Amen.

Marcus Borg, a sophisticated biblical scholar, wrote a deeply moving spiritual document titled, <u>Meeting Jesus Again for the First Time</u>. And this document tells of Borg's journey from the simplicity of a child's faith, through the complexity of a biblical scholar's search for truth, and then how he recovered his first love. Before it was too late, he realized that he had substituted knowledge, for the wisdom that comes from a personal relationship with God and so, he sought to remedy the situation, thus the name for his book: <u>Meeting Jesus Again for the First Time</u>.

You see, what makes our lives purposeful, authentic and influential is the sincerity of our search for wisdom. But, as our lesson unfolds, the contrast is very clear. There is a knowledge whose very appearance is deceptive. It appears to serve God, but as time goes on it proves to be false and foolish. James 3:13-16, shows what real godly wisdom is not. James writes: *Who is wise and understanding among you? Show by your good life that your works are done with gentleness born of wisdom. But if you have bitter envy and selfish ambition in your hearts, do not be boastful and false to the truth.*

Such wisdom does not come down from above, but is earthly, unspiritual, devilish. For where there is envy and selfish ambition, there will also be disorder and wickedness of every kind. And then in verses 17-18, we see what real wisdom from above produces. James continues: *But the wisdom from above is first pure, then peaceable, gentle, willing to yield, full of mercy and good fruits, without a trace of partiality or hypocrisy. It is a harvest of righteousness... sown in peace for those who make peace.*

James states that wisdom is both knowing and being. Faith in God produces more than exhortations and explanations; it also produces an example that is worthy to be followed. It's a wisdom that can be held accountable. The purpose of life is not knowledge, but it is wisdom put into responsible action. Notice how James introduces this portion of scripture with a question. *"Who is wise and understanding among you?"* he asks. Then, before we can even answer, he writes: It is those who *"do their works with gentleness born of wisdom."* Now, you know that we live in an "Age of Information" these days. We are constantly urged to tap into what the world calls wisdom. However, as James writes, there is a big difference between that kind of knowledge and wisdom that comes from above. The Bible has a great deal to say about wisdom, and it reveals the struggle between true wisdom and false teaching.

James is writing about teachers here, whose knowledge comes from a source outside of the kingdom and the principles of God. And, two of the characteristics of wisdom that comes from this source are arrogance and deceit. The same two characteristics we see in Lucifer, the Arch-angel, before his fall. But, a person who has discovered the wisdom from above, is not arrogant, but instead is humble. Or as one theologian put it: "The Grace of God humbles a person without degrading them – and exalts them without inflating them."[77] And, a person who has discovered the wisdom from above is not deceitful. Satan, the fallen angel is dark and deceitful, he comes only to steal, kill, and destroy. But Jesus, God in the flesh, is full of light and truth, and comes to offer Life.

Arrogance and boasting, seek to make us look better than we are. But on the other hand, wisdom from above is different. It is pure, peaceable, gentle and reasonable. It allows us to have a teachable spirit. It is full of mercy and contains no hypocrisy whatsoever.

There was once an old Arabian ruler who had three rather ungrateful but brilliant sons. As the old man lay dying, he called the sons into his bedroom to discuss their inheritance. "You will inherit my herd of camels," he said. The oldest son was to receive half of the herd, the middle son one third and the youngest son, one ninth. When the old man died, the sons met to divide up the herd. But, alas, there were 17 camels. There was no way to divide up a herd of 17 camels, one half, one third and one ninth, they thought. And so, the sons began fighting with one another. The fighting got worse. Gradually it infected the entire household, then the town, and then the Sheik's entire region. Finally, one day an older and wiser woman walked into town holding a rope attached to a single camel. "Here," she said quietly, "if it will stop the fighting, I will give you my camel and will divide your inheritance for you." The oldest son received nine camels; the middle son, six camels; the youngest, two camels. Everyone seemed pleased and content. Then they thought: $9 + 6 + 2 = 17$. And with just the hint of a smile on her face, the wise old woman picked up the rope from her camel and headed for home. Now, this woman had true wisdom going for her, she had a wisdom that was pure, peaceable, gentle and reasonable.

You know, Christians should be different from secular society. "We should seek wisdom from above", and if we will, it will show. May that be the trademark of your life, striving to seek wisdom from above that will show. Here's a great story. Once upon a time there was an old man who lived on the outskirts of town. He had lived there so long that no one knew who he was or where he had come from.

Some thought that he had been a very powerful king, but that was many years ago. Others suggested that he was once famous, rich, and generous, but he had lost everything. Still others said that he was once very wise and influential. There were even some who said he was holy. The children in the town, however, thought he was an old and stupid man and they made his life miserable. They threw stones at his windows, left dead animals on his front porch, destroyed his garden, and yelled nasty words at him at every opportunity. Then one day, one of the older boys came up with an idea to prove once and for all that those who thought he was a: Former king or rich, famous, and generous or wise and influential, and most especially, those who considered him holy were all wrong. No, he truly was just a stupid old man.

The boy knew how to catch a bird in a snare. He told his friends that he would catch the bird and together they would go to the old man's home and knock on the door. When the man would answer the boy would ask, "Old man, do you know what I have hidden behind my back?" Now he might guess that it is a bird, but with the second question I will get him. I will ask him if the bird is alive or dead. If he says dead, I will allow the bird to go free, but if he says the bird is alive, I will crush it to death with my hands. Either way he will prove he is only a stupid old man. The children thought it was a great plan. Thus, the older boy caught the bird and together they went off to the old man's house and knocked on the door. The man opened the door and seeing the large gathering of children realized something was up. The boy spoke quickly, "Old man, do you know what I have hidden behind my back?" The old man looked at the children one by one and out of the corner of his eye he saw a white feather fall to the ground. He answered, "Yes, I do. It's a white bird." The children's eyes grew large. How could he know it was a white bird? Maybe the people in town were right all along. But, the older boy was not to be deterred from his goal and quickly asked the second question. "Well that was a good guess, but is the bird alive or dead?"

Again, the old man looked with sad eyes at each of the children. Finally his eyes met those of the boy. He answered, "That depends on you; the answer is in your hands."[78] Now, certainly this old man was filled with wisdom and knowledge. Not only could he "outfox" the older boy at his own game, but he was wise enough to be able to teach them an important lesson at the same time.

You know, we have the choice to do good or evil. We have the chance to choose the wisdom of God or that of the world. Which will you choose?

Let me close with this, it's a short poem and it says a lot about our time on this earth. It goes like this: You're writing a "gospel," a chapter each day, by the deeds that you do, by the words that you say. People read what you write, whether faithless or true. So, what is the "gospel" according to you?

What is the gospel, the good news, according to you? Will your life be like a useless tunnel that can only sustain mushrooms, or will it be a life worthy of God's stamp of approval? You know, it's up to you, only time will tell. Amen.

God's Lenses

<u>Mark 2:13-22</u>

Jesus went out again beside the sea; the whole crowd gathered around him, and he taught them. As he was walking along, he saw Levi son of Alphaeus sitting at the tax booth, and he said to him, "Follow me." And he got up and followed him. And as he sat at dinner in Levi's house, many tax collectors and sinners were also sitting with Jesus and his disciples--for there were many who followed him. When the scribes of the Pharisees saw that he was eating with sinners and tax collectors, they said to his disciples, "Why does he eat with tax collectors and sinners?" When Jesus heard this, he said to them, "Those who are well have no need of a physician, but those who are sick; I have come to call not the righteous but sinners." Now John's disciples and the Pharisees were fasting; and people came and said to him, "Why do John's disciples and the disciples of the Pharisees fast, but your disciples do not fast?" Jesus said to them, "The wedding guests cannot fast while the bridegroom is with them, can they? As long as they have the bridegroom with them, they cannot fast. The days will come when the bridegroom is taken away from them, and then they will fast on that day. "No one sews a piece of unshrunk cloth on an old cloak; otherwise, the patch pulls away from it, the new from the old, and a worse tear is made. And no one puts new wine into old wineskins; otherwise, the wine will burst the skins, and the wine is lost, and so are the skins; but one puts new wine into fresh wineskins."

The title of the message this morning is: "God's Lenses." Think about that. Think, for a moment what it would be like to look through God's Lenses. Then compare the difference between what God would see and what the world sees.

The world sees "this life only." God sees "eternity." The world sees "an ancient book." God sees "His inspired Word." The world sees "religion." God sees "a personal relationship." The world sees "a prophet," "a teacher," "a good man." God sees "the Savior," "His only Son," "the King of kings," "Lord of lords," "The true Messiah," "The Way, the Truth and the Life." You know, things are much clearer when viewed from God's perspective. Whose lenses are you looking through?

Let us pray: May the words of my mouth and the meditations of each of our hearts be acceptable in Your sight, O God, our Rock and our Redeemer. Amen.

Today, in our reading, we hear Jesus telling a story about wineskins. He says that it would never be advisable to put new wine into old wineskins, because they have no elasticity. And since they can't expand with the pressure, they will eventually crack and the new wine will be lost. Now, in Jesus' days, wine was stored in animal skins that were supple, soft and elastic, capable of expanding when necessary. But, I think what Jesus was really trying to get at was the fact that human minds must be elastic enough to receive and contain new ideas, we need to be able to see things from a new perspective from God's perspective. Jesus offers to us, among other things, a new pair of glasses, through which to view the world. Why? Well, because the world's lenses don't allow us to see as God sees.

At some point, Old ways, Old manners, Old words, Old phrases, Old styles of worship and Old ways of expressing theology seem to come apart and crack. They simply grow brittle with time. Like old wineskins and they lose their elasticity. The early believers understood that and the church thrived. But, then somewhere along the way, the Church forgot Jesus' warning, that each generation must be diligent about pouring the new wine from one perishable vessel into another. The old wineskins must be discarded, while at-the-same-time the new wine, the message of Jesus Christ must be preserved.

You know, it's truly a pity that we would ever hold to something, that would allow the new wine of truth to be spilt. But we do. And so, Jesus' warning for the early church is just as relevant for us today. The new wine of the gospel should not be poured into the wineskins of the past.

Did you know that, people today are staying away from the church in droves? They are. Some are staying away from the church because they feel that it's just not relevant for them, some because the church in general, is sending the message that worship should always be a somber and serious thing and others because they just don't feel welcome in the churches of today. Here's a bit of information I find interesting. Market researchers report every year that more and more technologies, like cell phones and computers, come pre-loaded with video games on them. Why? Well, because more and more people, young and old, are giving themselves permission to have fun in their daily lives. In light of that thought let me share with you, a fun book titled "<u>101 Things to Do during a Dull Sermon</u>." Here are ten of their suggestions if you're bored: 1) Pass a note to the pianist asking whether she takes requests. 2) See if a yawn really is contagious. 3) Slap your neighbor. See if they turn the other cheek. 4) If they don't turn the other cheek, raise your hand and tell the pastor. 5) Devise ways of climbing into the balcony without using the stairs. 6) Listen for your pastor to use a word beginning with A then B then C and so on. 7) Sit in the back of the church and roll a handful of marbles under the pews ahead of you. After the service, credit yourself with 10 points for every marble that made it to the front. 8) Using church bulletins or visitor cards for raw materials, design, test, and modify a collection of paper airplanes. 9) Start from the back of the church and try to crawl all the way to the front without being noticed. 10) During a dull sermon, raise your hand and ask for permission to go to the rest room.[79]

You know, we wouldn't find that list so funny if we didn't relate to it. Sometimes we hear the words "Religion," or "Church," and we think "Boring," "Obligation," and "Duty." Sometimes, we forget the message of Psalm 16, which says: *"In God's presence there is not just joy… but fullness of joy."* A good example of "Joyful" vs. "Somber" worship comes from our passage today. Mark writes: *Some people came and asked Jesus, "How is it that John's disciples and the disciples of the Pharisees are fasting, but yours are not?"[80]* In other words, Jesus, how come Your disciples get to have fun and we don't? And Jesus answered: *"How can the guests of the bridegroom fast while He is with them? They cannot, so long as they have Him with them."* You see, the Pharisees, well, they were more intent on obeying rules than on understanding God. They wanted an outward expression of their inward sorrow. They wanted to say: "Look at me; I'm doing something righteous for God. And it's not so fun." They were looking through the lenses of the world, rather than through the lenses of God.

But, unlike the world, Jesus teaches that sincere worship flows from a sense of joy. Jesus explained: *"I have come that they might have life, and have it more abundantly."[81]* And in our reading today, He declares Himself to be the "life of the party," the Bridegroom. In effect, He says to them: "You are in the presence of God right now. Enjoy it. Get in on the party. Celebrate with Me while you have the chance." Jesus explained that His disciples didn't fast because there was no reason for them to fast while He was around. He wrapped His answer in the imagery of a wedding reception. He called Himself a bridegroom. Just as the mood of a wedding reception is one of celebration and joy, so also the mood of the followers of Jesus is to be full of joy. For the Christian, Jesus says, there is no reason to be sorrowful. Where there is death, I give life. Where there is guilt and separation from God, I bring forgiveness and oneness with the Father. Jesus has opened up the way of communication between God and us, and He is still there at the right hand of the Father; He is still there today, interceding for us.

Now, you might be thinking. Why is it that we still teach fasting in the church? Well, Jesus was not condemning fasting, in and of itself. No, instead He was condemning what motivated the religious people of His day to do what they did. Jesus Himself fasted and so did Paul and many others in the early Christian Church. They fasted in order to deepen their relationship with God. Do you see the difference? The motives are different. One is to draw attention to oneself and the other is to draw closer to God. Some of the legalists in the early church asked: *"Why don't your disciples fast?"* And Jesus answered, *"They cannot fast while the bridegroom is with them... this is a time to celebrate."* You see, part of the new wine is that worship and religion are not to be somber and sorrowful, but joyous and life-affirming. Jesus was all about life. He said: *"I come to bring Life and that more abundantly."* He also said: *"I am the way and the Truth and the Life."* And so worship in His name, is to be a time of celebration for the New Wine that His life, death and resurrection brings.

In an interview with a London newspaper, actor Christopher Walken revealed that he likes to bring a little fun to a movie set by pretending that it's his birthday. In the morning, as the makeup crew is preparing him for the shoot, he will act a little sad. Invariably, some kind-hearted makeup person will ask if he's feeling all right. He will mention off-handedly that today is his birthday, although it really isn't, and then swear them to secrecy. In a matter of hours, the cast and crew of the movie throw together a big birthday party for him, complete with cake and champagne or in the context of the church, New Wine. Everyone has a great time, and no one suspects that he planned the whole thing just to inject a little fun in his colleagues' day.[82] What a great idea! Who doesn't like a party, even if it is for no reason? It's sort of like receiving flowers from someone, for no reason at all. Think about it. If you're at work and you receive flowers. What happens? Everyone in the office asks: Is it you Birthday? Is it your anniversary? Is it a special day? And when you tell them: No, someone just sent flowers because they love me. Well, everyone goes, Oh! That is so, nice. You are so, blessed. It's like a party for no reason.

You know, we should never lose our taste for fun. It's life-affirming. It's like a revival. Jesus knew that. Jesus, while He walked this earth, revealed the nature and will of God, He revealed God's life-affirming nature. While the Jewish law of the Pharisees can only point out sin, Jesus Christ offers forgiveness of sin. That's why we celebrate. He didn't come to patch up the old religious system of Judaism with its rules and regulations. No, His purpose was to fulfill it by building a bridge between us and God, and also between us and others, so that we could celebrate God's gift of salvation together, as a community of faith. Because of Jesus' life and ministry, we who call ourselves by His name, can see more clearly the fact that God wants to bring all peoples of the world together one day, in joyful worship of Him.

You know, life is much clearer when viewed from God's perspective. The next time you are feeling out of sorts, or feel that things are just not going right. Stop for a moment and ask yourself, what lenses are you looking through, God's or the world's? My challenge for you today is this: To take off the lenses of the world and put on God's lenses. So that healing and the renewal of God's church can begin today, in this sanctuary, and then spread out into our community, our nation, and all around the world, until all see through new lenses, not just seeing "this life," but "eternity." Not just seeing "an ancient book," but "God's inspired Word." Not just seeing "religion," but "a personal relationship with God." Not seeing merely "a prophet," "a teacher," "a good man," but "The Savior," "God's only Son," "King of kings," "Lord of lords," "The true Messiah," "The Way, the Truth and the Life." That is God's plan for His created. It is His plan that all, will come to know and love Him. And the most exciting part is this, God allows us to work alongside Him in getting His message out. We are "ambassadors for Christ." We just need to make sure we are wearing the right lenses, God's lenses, so that all of our responses will be more loving, more joyful, more generous and, well, more Christ-like. That is our mission; that is God's mission for us. Amen.

God's Heart on Divorce

<u>Mark 10:2-16</u>
Some Pharisees came, and to test him they asked, "Is it lawful for a man to divorce his wife?" He answered them, "What did Moses command you?" They said, "Moses allowed a man to write a certificate of dismissal and to divorce her." But Jesus said to them, "Because of your hardness of heart he wrote this commandment for you. But from the beginning of creation, 'God made them male and female.' 'For this reason a man shall leave his father and mother and be joined to his wife, and the two shall become one flesh.' So they are no longer two, but one flesh. Therefore what God has joined together, let no one separate." Then in the house the disciples asked him again about this matter. He said to them, "Whoever divorces his wife and marries another, commits adultery against her; and if she divorces her husband and marries another, she commits adultery." People were bringing little children to him in order that he might touch them; and the disciples spoke sternly to them. But when Jesus saw this, he was indignant and said to them, "Let the little children come to me; do not stop them; for it is to such as these that the kingdom of God belongs. Truly I tell you, whoever does not receive the kingdom of God as a little child will never enter it." And he took them up in his arms, laid his hands on them, and blessed them.

A young woman named Sally was driving home from a business trip in Northern Arizona when she saw an elderly Navajo woman walking on the side of the road. As the trip was a long and quiet one, she stopped the car and asked the Navajo woman if she would like a ride. With a silent nod of thanks, the woman got into the car.

Resuming the journey, Sally tried in vain to make a bit of small talk with the Navajo woman, but the old woman just sat silently, looking intently at everything she saw, studying every little detail. Then the old woman noticed a brown bag on the seat next to Sally. "What's in the bag?" asked the old woman. Sally looked down at the brown bag and said: "It's a leather coat. I got it for my husband." The Navajo woman was silent for another moment or two. Then speaking with the quiet wisdom of an elder, she said: "Good trade." Marriage is one of the favorite themes of comedians these days. And that's no surprise, because relationships are difficult, particularly between men and women. One day Jesus was in Judea, when a great crowd came to Him. In that crowd were Pharisees who had decided to step forward and test Him, asking: *"Is it lawful for a man to divorce his wife?"* And Jesus responded: *"What did Moses command you?"* Well, the Pharisees knew the answer to that, and they said: *"Moses permitted a man to divorce his wife and send her away."* And then Jesus' responded with: *"It was because your hearts were hard that Moses wrote you that law."*

Now, there were two schools of thought in Jesus' day concerning divorce, one liberal and one conservative. Rabbi Shammai taught that divorce was only permissible on the grounds of some sexual impropriety. His was the stricter view. Rabbi Hillel, on the other hand, had a more liberal view and taught that a man could divorce his wife for any reason. If she burned his breakfast, put too much salt on his food, showed disrespect to him, spoke disrespectfully of her husband's parents in his presence, spoke to a man on the street, or even let her hair down in public, he could divorce her. The view of Rabbi Hillel was the view that was popular in Jesus' day. It was into this debate about divorce that the Pharisees wanted to lure Jesus, and trap Him, I think. They knew that whichever side He came down on, He was bound to alienate the folks on the other side.

Now, why do you think this biblical passage is so relevant for us today? Well, because people are still asking the same question: "Can a Christian man or woman divorce his or her spouse?"

In a day when many young marriages, and even many mature marriages, are coming apart at the seams, it is indeed a relevant question to ask.

"What did Moses command you?" Jesus asked. In other words: "What is the Old Testament view of this question?" Jesus asked the Pharisees. And when they answered correctly, Jesus responded: *It was because your hardness of hearts that Moses wrote you this law... At the beginning of creation God made them male and female. For this reason a man will leave his father and mother and be united to his wife, and the two will become one flesh. So they are no longer two, but one. Therefore what God has joined together, let no one separate.* In other words: Jesus says that marriage is serious business. You know, this is a difficult passage to preach on, because it provokes a variety of responses, in the hearts of its listeners, but, let me start here. The timing and location of where Jesus gave His commentary on divorce, in the Gospel of Mark, is critical to our understanding of it. Jesus had left Galilee, had crossed the Jordan River and was in the region of Perea. And it's not surprising that the Pharisees there, wanted to know what Jesus thought about divorce, because that was the region that was ruled by King Herod Antipas. You see, Herod just recently divorced his first wife to marry Herodias, the wife of his own brother.[83] And, it was this bizarre marriage that John the Baptist had criticized saying: *"It is not lawful for you to have your brother's wife."*[84] And it was because of this particular critique that John the Baptist lost his head, literally. And, since the Pharisees were "buddy-buddy" with the Herodians, we can picture them eagerly anticipating how Jesus might answer their question. If Jesus spoke for divorce, He would violate His own ethical principles. If He spoke against divorce, John's fate could be Jesus' fate. Possibly that was why they were so intent on "testing" Him that day. And here is another interesting fact. When we take a closer look at Jesus' statement: *"Whoever divorces his wife and marries another, commits adultery against her; and if she divorces her husband and marries another, she commits adultery against him."*

If we take this passage in its context, we find a very interesting connection. You see, the Greek used for the phrase "and marries" (*gameo*) is really better translated "to marry," or, "so as to marry." So, in other words, the passage is better translated: *"Whoever divorces his wife so as to marry another, commits adultery against her; and if she divorces her husband so as to marry another, she commits adultery against him,"* which is exactly what King Herod had done.

Now, Jesus was very strong on marriage to one person, "until death do they part." But, when we speak of a Christian position on divorce, we must recognize that there are certain circumstances, under which a person simply must be permitted to divorce. Even Jesus said that, according to Matthew. According to Matthew, Jesus said: *"If you leave your wife, unless there is adultery, [so as to] marry another woman, you yourself are committing adultery."*[85] Why? Because adultery itself is the divorce. Adultery is the thing that breaks the bond of marriage. Just as an excommunication merely recognizes the fact that someone has already been removed from the people, a divorce merely legalizes what harlotry has created.[86] And then later, the apostle Paul speaking of a marriage between a believer and an unbeliever, says: *If an unbelieving partner wishes to leave the relationship, let it be so; in such a case the believing brother or sister is not bound. For it is to peace that God has called the believing spouse.*[87] You know, we must never forget that our Lord had immense sympathy for those who were suffering. When He dealt with people, it was never on the basis of Law, but always on the basis of Love. He ate and drank with sinners. He saved an adulterous woman from being stoned. He even forgave the soldiers who crucified Him. And when He met a Samaritan woman at a well, a woman who had had five husbands and who was currently living with a man who was not her husband, He did not treat her with contempt.

I think Jesus would say that because of the fallen-ness of humanity, divorce will happen and sometimes it is even the lesser of two evils. But, I think He also knew of the immense suffering that always goes along with a divorce. In divorce, men suffer, women suffer and especially, children suffer. And it may be no accident that in Mark, immediately after Jesus talks about divorce, we see Him calling the little children and putting His arms around them. And so, even though the Church never welcomes divorce, we have come to realize that in some instances, it is better for certain marriages to come to an end. Especially in an abusive relationship, that is beyond reconciliation. Jesus would never advocate that a person suffer in that way.

You know, this is not just a secular problem. Many people in our churches are divorcing at an alarming rate. The United Methodist Church recognizes that as stated in our Social Principles. The words we find there are these: We grieve over the devastating emotional, spiritual, and economic consequences of divorce for all involved and are concerned about high divorce rates.[88] It also states that: When a married couple is estranged beyond reconciliation, even after thoughtful consideration and counsel, divorce is a regrettable alternative.[89] Yes, even Christians struggle with divorce. But there is hope. And that hope is to be found in God's church. There is something we, as God's people, can do.

First, we can acknowledge that there is immense suffering in every divorce. And second, and more importantly, we can acknowledge that there is hope to be found as a divorced person calls upon God's restoring and healing power. And third, the church of today can repent from its past alienation of divorced brothers and sisters in Christ. And, instead, we can offer to them forgiveness, reconciliation, and most importantly, God's healing love. After divorce, there is great suffering and grief; it is not, as some think, the easy way out. I have yet to meet a divorced person who did not go through tremendous grief.

Some have even said that divorce is worse than losing a spouse by death, because it's like a "living death." After divorce, there is always a great sense of loss by all involved. Even people coming out of horrendous situations grieve, not for the loss of the abuse that they may have suffered in that broken relationship, but for the loss of the "dream" that they had for that relationship. But in God's awesome power and with the help of the church, that person's life can be reworked, remolded and reshaped into one that is even more beautiful than it was before the tragedy happened. That's the wonderful hope we have in Christ.

In closing let me say this. There are no perfect marriages. In spite of what you might have heard, no marriage is truly made in heaven. Good marriages are made through a lot of give-and-take here on earth. No, there are no perfect marriages but there can be great ones. Those are the marriages in which two people have committed themselves to God and to one another, to work through their struggles in a Christ-like way. Those are the marriages in which two people have committed themselves to love one another, with God's help. Those are the marriages that will thrive and not only thrive, but also bring glory to God. Have you ever thought about your marriage bringing glory to God? It does, as far as it reflects "as in a mirror dimly," the future Perfect marriage, between Christ and His Bride, the Church.

And even though it is a mystery to us right now, on this present earth, it won't always be that way. No, one day, one day the New Jerusalem filled with all who are in Christ, the New Jerusalem, the Bride of Christ, will "come down out of Heaven from God and all who are in that city will dwell on the New Earth, with God, forever."[90] And, all that glorifies God in our relationships, on this present earth, will continue then and throughout eternity. So be it. Amen.

An Over Abundance

<u>John 6:1-21</u>
After this Jesus went to the other side of the Sea of Galilee, also called the Sea of Tiberias. A large crowd kept following him, because they saw the signs that he was doing for the sick. Jesus went up the mountain and sat down there with his disciples. Now the Passover, the festival of the Jews, was near. When he looked up and saw a large crowd coming toward him, Jesus said to Philip, "Where are we to buy bread for these people to eat?" He said this to test him, for he himself knew what he was going to do. Philip answered him, "Six months' wages would not buy enough bread for each of them to get a little." One of his disciples, Andrew, Simon Peter's brother, said to him, "There is a boy here who has five barley loaves and two fish. But what are they among so many people?" Jesus said, "Make the people sit down." Now there was a great deal of grass in the place; so they sat down, about five thousand in all. Then Jesus took the loaves, and when he had given thanks, he distributed them to those who were seated; so also the fish, as much as they wanted. When they were satisfied, he told his disciples, "Gather up the fragments left over, so that nothing may be lost." So they gathered them up, and from the fragments of the five barley loaves, left by those who had eaten, they filled twelve baskets. When the people saw the sign that he had done, they began to say, "This is indeed the prophet who is to come into the world." When Jesus realized that they were about to come and take him by force to make him king, he withdrew again to the mountain by himself. When evening came, his disciples went down to the sea, got into a boat, and started across the sea to Capernaum. It was now dark, and Jesus had not yet come to them. The sea became rough because a strong wind was blowing. When they had rowed about three or four miles, they saw Jesus walking on the sea and coming near the boat, and they were terrified. But he said to them, "It is I; do not be afraid." Then they wanted to take him into the boat, and immediately the boat reached the land toward which they were going.

There is a certain rock known as a geode. From the outside it is a dull-looking stone. Yet crack it open and you discover a breathtaking array of crystals in a hollow core. Sometimes, I feel like I'm holding an un-cracked geode in my hands when I look at a Bible text. I know there is a powerful blessing in the passage. It must simply be opened by the power of the Holy Spirit. So, as we examine the text, it is my prayer that God will shed some extraordinary light that will be useful for us here today.

Let us pray: May the words of my mouth and the meditations of each of our hearts be acceptable in Your sight, O God, our Rock and our Redeemer. Amen.

There was a need. Our text begins with a human need. Jesus had been busily ministering from Jerusalem to Galilee. And the healings, the preaching, the conflict had left Him very tired. So He got into a boat with His disciples and sailed across the lake to take a break. But the crowds of people had not had enough of the Master's words and deeds. They wanted more. So they tramped around the lake's north shore, perhaps a distance of fifteen or twenty miles, in order to be where Jesus was.

The text tells us it was the time of Passover. That would mean that the roads would have been filled with people on their way to Jerusalem. How quickly word spread of Jesus and His whereabouts. And so it was that the crowd swelled as men, women, and children detoured to have a good look at Him. So, there stands Jesus atop a hillside overlooking Lake Galilee, around supper-time. But, wait, there's more need than for a meal. There are sick people in the crowd. So, too, are the lonely, the adulterous, the confused, the lost and the misguided. That day, Jesus saw a needy crowd.

But today, think about this, today, through modern mass communication we literally see more needy crowds than people did in Jesus day. Today we see so many hurts that we can do so little about, and we feel powerless. So we avert our eyes, we stop our ears to the cries for help, and we grow calloused in our hearts. The result is the poor hurting masses become increasingly invisible to us.

But that doesn't do away with the fact that we have the needy right here among us, the orphans and the widows. Who are the orphans? Who are the widows? Well the orphans are literally the children without parents, but also, the latch-key kids, the children who are left alone much of the day, so that food can be put on the table in the evening. And the widows, well of course, they are the women who have outlived their spouses. But let's not forget the others. I think we need to understand that this is a group that is increasingly made up of single moms, refugees from war-torn relationships, single moms who are trying their best to keep all the plates spinning like a weary circus performer: Working full-time or more... Paying the bills... Doing the laundry... Helping with the homework... Making the school meetings... Being the chauffeur... Cooking the meals... Cleaning the house... Being both mother and father to the children... Not to mention the grueling task of trying to put the shattered pieces of their family life and their own heart back together. Especially, especially, the needs of single moms require of us the same overabundance of compassion that Jesus showed to the weary crowds that day.

You know, it is so easy to see and not see, to hear and not hear, to become so self-absorbed in what we want that we miss what others need. I mean, open your eyes. We each pass by more hurting people, more potential ministry in a single day than any one person could do in a lifetime. There on the hillside where you stand, do you see the throngs of hurting people all around you? Jesus did. If not, ask Him to open your eyes to the lost in your own neighborhood, in your place of work, at your family gatherings, in this congregation.

Now, in our story, there was an inadequacy. Notice the text reveals how Christ had set up this situation and used it to test Philip. John tells us that Philip was from this region. He knew the towns, the valleys, the roads and the lake. He would have also known what local resources could be brought to bear on the needs, so Jesus asked him: *"How are we to buy bread so that these people may eat?"* And Philip did the math in his head. Then, standing beside Jesus he looked at the hillside crowd, surveyed the contents of his own pockets, and declared his resources woefully inadequate. Jesus tested Philip that day. And, I think, He was educating His disciples to do what they could do and leave the rest to God. He was illustrating a scriptural law. Additional resources and powers are given to those who use what resources and powers they already have. To those who use their talents, more will be given. To those who do not use their talents, all will be taken away. So, Philip flunks the test. He doesn't have the over abundance of compassion for the crowds like Jesus.

But there is another disciple, Andrew. Andrew does have the compassion of Christ. Andrew sees the crowd, the hunger, the expense, and he sees Jesus. To be sure he sees the daunting task, but he also sees a way to begin. Andrew had the capacity to say: "I am only one. I can't do everything. But I can do something. And just because I can't do everything, I will not fail to do that which I can do." So, Jesus performs a miracle. He receives the fish and bread, and we hear that the crowd ate until they were "filled;" in the Greek they were literally "so full they could eat no more." And so, Philip, Andrew, the other disciples, the little child, and the multitudes, all learned of God's over abundance of compassion that day. And they also learned that God can do a lot with a little. They learned that little is much when God is in it. They learned not to look at the multitudes or the lack or what lines one's own pockets. They learned to look at Jesus, to give Him what they could and to leave the rest to God.

Jesus Christ can take the commonest bread and pickled fish, bless and multiply them, and make a banquet for 5,000. Now, that's a miracle. And another miracle is when God Almighty takes any one of us, a hopeless sinner, washes away our sins, fills us with His Holy Spirit, and makes us a blessing to others. That's salvation and what it means to be a Christian. You see, it is not what we are, in and of ourselves. It is what God does in us and through us that makes the difference. God can receive our faith, and our lives, inadequate as we are, and make us enough on every hillside in every land, in every generation.

I like the story about a man who was hiking to a remote village in Peru. Maybe you have heard it before. He found a rock along the road, and put it in his pack as a souvenir. That evening he strode into the village to a very unfriendly welcome. No one offered him a bed. No one asked him to sit by their fire. Why, because a famine had troubled the Indians for over a month. And the people were starving. Each was simply afraid to share the little they had. Then he got an idea and said: "I'm going to make some stone soup. Ummm. It's tasty. I grew up on it. And you'll like it a lot." Then he opened his back pack and produced the rock he'd found that morning. One Indian objected: "Stone soup. Why that's the stupidest thing I've ever heard." "Trust me," the man said. "See. I've brought the stone. But I'm going to need a pot to put it in." An Indian woman quickly volunteered her pot. "And I'll need about two large buckets of water to boil the stone in." A man quickly brought water. So, in went the stone, in went the water, and over the fire, the pot was suspended. Curious, now, the villagers began to gather around the pot, peering into its contents. The man began to stir the pot and drool. "You know, stone soup sure is good with carrots!" To which an Indian said: "I've got six carrots." He quickly fetched them and they were cut up into the pot. Then the man smelled deeply of the bubbly broth and sighed: "Some potatoes sure would add to the flavor." From pockets and other hiding places came dozens of spuds. They were quickly added to the soup.

Soon people were bringing onions, celery, and bits of meat to top off the pot of stone soup. And within the hour a community formed around that stew pot. All ate. And all were filled.[91] Now what we have here are people giving the little they have, coming together as a team, so that all could benefit. Some suggest that something like this happened that day on the hillside with Jesus. But that is not what the text tells us. No, what the disciples saw on the hillside that day was a divine act of God, a miracle. So, the moral of the story is this: People can be encouraged to come together to help one another, but so much more can happen when God's miraculous power is added to that. Do you see the difference? Both are good, but one is better. There is a big difference when you add God's miraculous power to a situation.

Our story ends with the disciples crossing the lake again, this time without Jesus. They are afraid, but then Jesus comes walking on the water and when they look to Him and want Him there with them, *"immediately the boat reaches the shore"* and all is well. The next time you see a need and feel inadequate for the task, as the disciples did: Don't look at the magnitude of the crowd, or the laws of nature, look to Christ. Don't count the difficulties presented; look at what God can do. Don't measure your problems; measure God's power.

I like what Charles Swindoll says about certain laws of nature. He says: TAKE GRAVITY. Heavy objects fall toward the earth. Always. So a builder can construct a house and never worry about his materials floating away. Count on it. TAKE CHEMISTRY. Mixing certain elements in precise proportions yields the same result. Always. So a doctor can prescribe a medication with predictable confidence. TAKE ASTRONOMY. The sun, the moon, those stars work in perfect harmony. Always. Even the mysterious eclipse comes as no surprise. TAKE ANATOMY. Whether it's the pupil of the eye expanding and contracting in response to light, or our skin regulating our body temperature, or our built-in response to breathe in and breathe out every few seconds, it's all so predictable.

We operate, every day, on the basis of the laws of nature as we know them.[92] And because of that, when a miracle is needed, we too, like the disciples, are tempted to ask: "Jesus, what do you mean, give them something to eat? Send the people home. We can't take care of them today." But, you know what? God is not subject to the laws and facts that govern the world as we are. Now, He doesn't always override natural law, as we know it. But what I suggest to you today is that, where Jesus is present no fact, no matter how indisputable, will keep God from accomplishing His plan through everyday Christians like you and me. God can and will, turn the smallest of offerings, given in faith, into an over abundance of whatever is needed. Will you trust Him on that?

You know, God is more than able. When the disciples looked to Christ and wanted Him in the boat with them, "Immediately they reached the shore", they reached their destination. Jesus is the pacesetter. He is out in front of us all the time, minutes ahead, sizing up the situation, providing the solutions before we even know what the problems are. He is the Messiah, the Almighty One. With Him as our partner, there is no such thing as an offering that is, too little or too insignificant, to make a difference. So, when you feel that tug on your heart, when God calls you to a task, remember Jesus Christ is with you, preparing the way, and standing ready to multiply your offerings. You can count on Him. Amen.

He Loves Us Into Life

<u>Mark 5:21-43</u>
When Jesus had crossed again in the boat to the other side, a great crowd gathered around him; and he was by the sea. Then one of the leaders of the synagogue named Jairus came and, when he saw him, fell at his feet and begged him repeatedly, "My little daughter is at the point of death. Come and lay your hands on her, so that she may be made well, and live." So he went with him. And a large crowd followed him and pressed in on him. Now there was a woman who had been suffering from hemorrhages for twelve years. She had endured much under many physicians, and had spent all that she had; and she was no better, but rather grew worse. She had heard about Jesus, and came up behind him in the crowd and touched his cloak, for she said, "If I but touch his clothes, I will be made well." Immediately her hemorrhage stopped; and she felt in her body that she was healed of her disease. Immediately aware that power had gone forth from him, Jesus turned about in the crowd and said, "Who touched my clothes?" And his disciples said to him, "You see the crowd pressing in on you; how can you say, 'Who touched me?'" He looked all around to see who had done it. But the woman, knowing what had happened to her, came in fear and trembling, fell down before him, and told him the whole truth. He said to her, "Daughter, your faith has made you well; go in peace, and be healed of your disease." While he was still speaking, some people came from the leader's house to say, "Your daughter is dead. Why trouble the teacher any further?" But overhearing what they said, Jesus said to the leader of the synagogue, "Do not fear, only believe." He allowed no one to follow him except Peter, James, and John, the brother of James. When they came to the house of the leader of the synagogue, he saw a commotion, people weeping and wailing loudly. When he had entered, he said to them, "Why do you make a commotion and weep?

The child is not dead but sleeping." And they laughed at him. Then he put them all outside, and took the child's father and mother and those who were with him, and went in where the child was. He took her by the hand and said to her, "Talitha cum," which means, "Little girl, get up!" And immediately the girl got up and began to walk about (she was twelve years of age). At this they were overcome with amazement. He strictly ordered them that no one should know this, and told them to give her something to eat.

On Thursday we will be celebrating Thanksgiving. It will be a day when most of us will gather with friends and family around a great Thanksgiving meal. But there is something we should not forget that day. We should not forget the source of all the good things for which we are thankful.

Let us pray: May the words of my mouth and the meditations of each of our hearts be acceptable in Your sight, O God, our Rock and our Redeemer. Amen.

Jesus had attained celebrity status. People were coming from all around to hear Him teach. And, more to the point, they were coming to Him for healing. We can understand that. There were no reliable doctors in that time. No MRI's. No CAT scans. Not even X-rays. No, the people who were desperate for help felt they had no place to turn. But then word got out about a man whose very presence brought healing. So, quite naturally, the people rushed to Him and reached out to Him. And, of course, He responded. Many were healed. And then, even more people came. By the thousands they came. And they pressed in around Him, seeking to receive His healing power.

In the middle of the crowd was a woman who had been sick for twelve years. What that meant for her was that no one was supposed to touch her as long as the illness continued.

How sad. How uncomfortable. How humiliating. Her condition would prevent her from getting married. She wasn't even supposed to go into the temple for worship or religious instruction. She was despised by all around her. And there was no one who could help her. Mark, the Gospel writer, tells us that *"she had suffered a great deal under the care of many doctors and had spent all she had, yet instead of getting better she grew worse."* The doctors had taken her money, yet had not given her any relief. So, here she was impoverished, outcast, and without hope. Until, she comes to Jesus. She had heard that He was the physician she had been looking for. There she was in the middle of the crowd, in a delicate situation, to say the least. She couldn't cry out about her condition. No one was supposed to even touch her. How can they help but touch her in a crowd like that? "Unclean! Unclean!" was what she was supposed to cry out. But, she might even get hurt. Who knows what an angry crowd might do to such a woman? She couldn't risk speaking up and having Jesus reach out to touch her. And so, she thought to herself: If I can just get close enough to touch Him, just touch the hem of His garment, then I will be healed. Probably He won't even know. But He does know. Jesus always knows.

You've got a problem, you've got a need. Jesus knows. You kneel down by your bed and pour you heart out over some situation that seems hopeless, Jesus knows. You take your deep concern to God, He knows. This woman came up behind Jesus and touched His cloak. Immediately she was healed and was freed from her suffering. And Jesus knew. He turned around in the crowd and said: *"Who touched Me?"* The disciples were amazed at Jesus' statement. *"You see the people crowding against You,"* they said, *"and yet You ask: 'Who touched Me?'"* But Jesus kept looking around to see who had done it. The woman is mortified. She thought she could hide in the crowd, but it didn't work. She's been found out, exposed. Mark then tells us: *"Then the woman... came and fell at His feet and, trembling with fear, told Him the whole truth."*

He speaks to her. "Daughter," He says. She was a very young woman. *"Daughter, your faith has made you well. Go in peace and be freed from your suffering."*

"Be freed from your suffering." Be freed physically. Be freed socially. Be freed spiritually. Be freed! What a beautiful and important story of faith this is. Father John Powell, the author of a book titled: <u>Through The Eyes of Faith</u>, tells about his prison ministry. About once a month, he visited a prisoner in the state penitentiary. He described how difficult that was for him personally, the atmosphere was dismal, dark and depressing. However, on one occasion, Father Powell said he had an enlightening experience in that dark, dismal and depressing prison environment. An elderly woman was standing beside him as they moved through the visitor line. Together, they went through numerous security checkpoints. They were required to produce identification; they were required to pass through metal detectors; they were led by heavily armed guards through countless doors made of strong steel bars. And through it all, Powell said he could not help but notice how this sweet, dear woman was smiling warmly toward everyone, waving tenderly to the guards and calling many of them by name, and greeting everyone in a kind and loving way. Powell was fascinated with her. She was absolutely radiant. She was a ray of sunshine and a breath of fresh air in that sullen place.

Suddenly, he said to her: "I'll bet you bring a lot of love into this world with your smiling face and kind words." "Father," she replied: "I decided a long time ago that there are no strangers in my world, only brothers and sisters." Reflecting on that experience, Powell wrote this remarkable paragraph. Listen closely. He says: "That lady drew out of me a deep and warm reaction of love. And gradually I came to realize that people are not only one thing, good or bad, but many things. In every human being there are things like: Warmth, love, affection, but there are also things like: Hurt, anger and weakness.

We stimulate or draw out of them one or the other. It all depends upon our approach, and our approach depends upon our attitude." And then Powell writes these concluding words: This was the genius of Jesus. He took people where they were and loved them into life. This is precisely what Jesus did for, those whose lives He touched. He was a living portrait of love in action.[93]

Jesus that day replied with one of the most mysterious statements that day when He sensed that someone had touched Him. He said: *"I felt power flow from Me."* What an interesting statement that is. I wonder what exactly happened in that moment. Did the lady drain His battery? It sounds as though He is almost describing a power surge. *"I felt power flow from Me,"* He said. Well, whatever happened, the important thing, of course, is that in the midst of the crowd, Christ felt the touch of a single person. You know, we can never say that in the vastness of the universe that God doesn't care about our concerns. Not only does God care, He actually solicits our concerns: *"Come unto me,"* He says, *"all who are weary and are carrying heavy burdens, and I will give you rest."* Jesus calls us into His presence to rest in His loving arms when we are feeling weary from this life.

One pastor writes about his seminary training. He says: When I was in seminary, there was on staff a psychologist named Dr. Charles Gurkin. He was quite renowned within his field, having written several books. And all the students were required to take a course from him. I will never forget what he said to us one day. He said, no minister will ever get close to a person who he or she is unwilling to physically touch. If you are not willing to touch a person, you, psychologically, are unwilling to minister to them. And then the pastor commented: This particularly came close to me when I had a church member in the hospital with a highly contagious disease. I was told by the nurse at the desk that I should put on rubber gloves to go into his room. "Are these necessary?" I asked. The nurse replied: "I work with these patients all day and I would not think of going into one of the rooms without wearing gloves."

Well, I thought, she is the expert not me, so I put on the latex gloves. When I entered his room he immediately extended his hand, and when I reciprocated that glove was very obvious. Frankly, I was embarrassed and I apologized for it. When I went home that day I remembered the words of Dr. Gerkin: You will never draw close to a person who you are unwilling to physically touch. In future trips to the hospital, the gloves came off. I simply felt that I could not be Christ's representative in that situation unless there was direct contact, like a touch from the Master's hand.[94] We hear that Jesus touches not only the woman, who was considered unclean, but also, a young girl who was already dead. Jesus knew of the healing power of a touch and He never hesitated to utilize that power.

In our story, with whom do you identify? There are plenty of people here. There's a woman whose whole life has been caught and dominated by a life-threatening illness. There's a distraught father. There's a little girl whose young life has been cut short. There are the disciples who don't know what to think about all of this. Where are you?

There also is another face, the strong, life-giving face of Jesus, Who says to us: "Get up!" Get up, go and touch someone else and through My power love them back into life, as well. Sometimes it's not easy to reach out and touch someone who needs the healing power of the Lord. But strangely enough, in other situations, the temptation to touch is almost overwhelming: Despite the "Do Not Touch" signs, a museum was having no success in keeping people from touching – and soiling – priceless furniture and art. But the problem evaporated overnight when a clever museum employee replaced the signs with ones that read: "Caution: Wash Hands After Touching!"[95]

On one occasion Dr. Fred Craddock said: When I was living in Atlanta, I heard about a young man in his early twenties dying, in the hospital. This man had no church connection, but someone said he had relatives who had been in the church. So they called a minister from that church, and he went to the hospital. The young man was almost dead, and the minister came, stood out in the hall, and asked them to open the door. When they opened the door, he yelled in a prayer. Another minister heard about it and rushed to the hospital, went into the room, and pulled up a chair and lifted his head and cradled it in her arm. She sang. She quoted scripture. She prayed. She sang. She quoted scripture. She prayed. And he died. After that, some of her seminary friends said: "Weren't you scared? His illness was contagious." And she said, "Of course I was scared." "Well then, why did you do it," they asked? And she said, "I just imagined if Jesus had gotten the call, what He would've done. I had to go," she said.[96] There is no way to do the work of Christ in this world without touching. I believe that God calls all of us to reach out and touch others. Why do I feel that way? Well, I think one song writer said it best when he wrote: He touched me, O He touched me. And, O the joy that floods my soul; something happened and now I know, He touched me and made me whole.[97] That's what Jesus did for me. Before that time, I had no hope. I was "shackled by a heavy burden," of fear, restlessness and a sense that life just didn't have much purpose. But after His healing touch, I was freed from all of that. He touched me and brought into my heart new Life, literally. And for that I am thankful. Maybe you can remember a time when He did the same for you.

You know, almost every Thanksgiving gathering allows for a time of sharing, a time when we name the things for which we are thankful. So, this is my challenge to you this year. My challenge to you is, to remember that time when Jesus touched your heart and then share that experience, with your family and loved ones, this Thursday, when you are given the opportunity to share what you are most thankful for. Amen.

A Great Thanksgiving

<u>Ephesians 1: 1-14</u>
Paul, an apostle of Christ Jesus by the will of God, To the saints who are in Ephesus and are faithful in Christ Jesus: Grace to you and peace from God our Father and the Lord Jesus Christ. Blessed be the God and Father of our Lord Jesus Christ, who has blessed us in Christ with every spiritual blessing in the heavenly places, just as he chose us in Christ before the foundation of the world to be holy and blameless before him in love. He destined us for adoption as his children through Jesus Christ, according to the good pleasure of his will, to the praise of his glorious grace that he freely bestowed on us in the Beloved. In him we have redemption through his blood, the forgiveness of our trespasses, according to the riches of his grace that he lavished on us. With all wisdom and insight he has made known to us the mystery of his will, according to his good pleasure that he set forth in Christ, as a plan for the fullness of time, to gather up all things in him, things in heaven and things on earth. In Christ we have also obtained an inheritance, having been destined according to the purpose of him who accomplishes all things according to his counsel and will, so that we, who were the first to set our hope on Christ, might live for the praise of his glory. In him you also, when you had heard the word of truth, the gospel of your salvation, and had believed in him, were marked with the seal of the promised Holy Spirit; this is the pledge of our inheritance toward redemption as God's own people, to the praise of his glory.

Around Thanksgiving, many people try to focus on the things for which they are thankful. Now, I don't know how you are doing on your thankfulness list, but this I do know, there is something is more important than the list. And that is from whence comes all the things we have to be thankful for.

Michael Bausch tells a great story about an archaeologist named Howard Carter. In 1922 Carter was completing nearly fifteen years of digging in the famous Valley of the Kings in Egypt. He was hoping to find the royal tomb of a famous Pharaoh, Tutankhamen. But, his days of digging were coming to an end, money was running out, and they had found nothing. That is, until they discovered sixteen stairs leading into the earth. Thousands of baskets filled with rocks and sand had to be carried away, but eventually a door was found at the end of a long passageway. Carter drilled a small hole in the door and stuck an iron-testing rod into a dark, blank space. He then inserted a candle into the hole and peered in. As his eyes grew accustomed to the light, details emerged into his view, and he saw strange animals, statues, and the glint of gold, everywhere. And for a moment he was struck dumb with amazement. Until someone asked, "Can you see anything?" And Carter replied, "Yes, wonderful things."[98] The apostle Paul gives us some reasons we can look towards Thanksgiving and see wonderful things. First of all, he says we are blessed. He writes: *Praise be to the God and Father of our Lord Jesus Christ, who has blessed us in the heavenly realms with every spiritual blessing in Christ.* Is there anyone in this room who feels blessed?

A certain king had two servants. To one he said: "I want you to travel for six months through my kingdom and bring back a sample of every weed you can find." To another the king said: "I want you to travel through my kingdom for six months and bring back a sample of every flower you can find." Six months later, both servants stood before the king. To both, the king asked: "Have you carried out my command?" The first servant answered: "I have, and I was amazed to find there were so many weeds in the kingdom. In fact there are, nothing but weeds in this kingdom!" And the second servant also answered: "I have, and I am amazed how many beautiful flowers there are in the kingdom. In fact there are, nothing but beautiful flowers in this kingdom!" Now, these two servants each found what they were looking for.

So do we, and if you are seeing only weeds in your life, let me ask you this: Are there no blessings in your life? Do you have no one who loves you? Is there no beauty outside your window, no strength left in your body? Do you have no mind to guide you to new fun things or new opportunities, no faith to bear you up when circumstance weighs you down? Are you really without resources to make this next week or month or year a wonderful one? Count your blessings, says the old hymn.

In *Leadership Magazine* Mark Tidd tells about an old man who came to the house that was being rented out to a group of college kids. The old man's eyes were glassy and his face glistened with silver stubble. He carried a wicker basket filled with a few unappealing vegetables. He bid the students a good morning and then offered his produce for sale. And because they were uneasy and thinking that maybe he was intoxicated, they made a quick purchase to get rid of him. But to their chagrin, he returned the next week, introducing himself as Mr. Roth, the man who lived in the old shack down the road. And at that time, their fears subsided, because they got close enough to realize it wasn't alcohol but cataracts that marbleized his eyes. On future visits, he would shuffle in, wearing two mismatched right shoes, and pull out a harmonica. With glazed eyes set on a future glory, he'd puff out old gospel tunes between conversations about vegetables and religion. The students really began to like him and wanted to help him. On one visit, he exclaimed, "The Lord is so good! I came out of my house this morning and found a bag full of shoes and clothing on my porch." "That's wonderful, Mr. Roth!" the students said, "We're happy for you." "You know what's even more wonderful?" he asked. "Just yesterday I met some people that could use them." You know, no matter our situation, we can always count our blessings.

Paul says we are blessed, he also says, we are chosen. *For God chose us in Him before the creation of the world to be holy and blameless in His sight.* You and I have been chosen. You have been chosen. What a beautiful word that is - chosen.

Can you ever remember the agony of not being chosen? Is there anybody in the room who was ever the last to be chosen for kickball? Anyone who did not make the cheerleading squad or volley ball team? Anyone ever sat on the bench while someone else got the glory? Well, this time you and I are not left out. We have been chosen.

Several years ago, a California aerospace company hired a motivational consultant to examine and stimulate its work force. The consultant interviewed one of the senior vice presidents who told him about a particular section where production and performance were extremely high. Turnover and absenteeism in this department were the lowest in the company. Morale was very high. What seemed to puzzle the executive was that the work done there was mechanical and repetitive. This group of employees maintained the pipes in the plant. Their job was checking temperatures and pressures. The delicacy of the equipment meant that the pipes had to work within strict tolerances or there would be expensive damage. But why was morale so high? The consultant visited the department and the foreman took him on a tour. The consultant noticed that all the workers wore green surgical smocks. He asked the foreman about it. The foreman explained that he got them from his son, a cardiovascular surgeon. The consultant said, "Ah, so you wear them for comfort." "No, no!" the foreman said, "It's because we are surgeons. Just like my son. He takes care of the pipes of the body. We take care of the pipes of the plant! The plant isn't going to have any breakdowns as long as we're working on its arteries. We take care of these pipes exactly the way a doctor takes care of your heart." The consultant even noticed that there were names on the locker doors which said, "Doctor" and then the worker's name.[99] What was happening here? Well, the workers in that maintenance department understood their work was important, just like a doctor's work is important. They felt privileged doing what they were doing. They felt chosen. It makes a difference when someone feels chosen.

You probably know that a large percentage of so-called "acting out" in small children is simply their way of getting "noticed." When they cannot get the attention they want any other way, they do something guaranteed to drive their parents up the wall. Well, one mom tells of putting her young son to bed for the umpteenth time. Her patience was worn thin. When she heard him cry "Mama" again, she yelled to him, "If you call Mama one more time, I'll spank you!" After that there was quiet. Then, just as she sat down, she heard a wee whisper, "Mrs. Green, may I have a drink of water?"[100] Now, was it really water her son was calling for or was it her attention? Every parent knows the answer to that, they want to be noticed. And it's not just children. Do you know what the most common complaint is that spouses have against each other? Invariably, "not being noticed," heads the list. Many people have had it with being taken for granted in the home and in the office and, perhaps, even in the church. Everyone in this world has a need to feel like he or she counts. Thus it is with great joy that we hear the words from the Scripture, *"we are chosen!"*

Finally, Paul says we are destined. *God destined us to be adopted as His sons and daughters through Jesus Christ, in accordance with His pleasure and will.* He "intended" for us to be, or "designed" us to be adopted as His sons and daughters through belief in Jesus Christ. Now, we could trip all over that word "destined." One pastor described the difference between Methodists and Presbyterians like this. He said: The Presbyterian church believes in predestination, that everything which is going to happen was planned by the Almighty at the beginning of time, and that we cannot alter God's plan.'[101] But to that, I say, the Methodist church and I am pretty sure the Baptist church, rejects at least the "election" part of predestination. By this I mean that our traditional Methodist/Baptist beliefs hold to the fact, that God does not choose, ahead of time, some for eternal salvation and others not.

D. L. Moody tried to resolve the conflict between predestination and human freedom like this: "I come to the door of salvation and see written over it "Whosoever will, may come." Then as I enter the door, and turn around, it says, "Chosen in Christ before the foundation of the world." You know what? I have no question about God's ultimate desire for us all. God wants us to be adopted into His family, through faith in Jesus Christ. And when we accept, through faith, the plan God has for us, to be members of His own family we come to see ourselves as God wants us to be, "children of God." God's perfect plan is that we will walk through that door, and thus be chosen and adopted into His family.

So, as we look toward Thanksgiving this year, shouldn't we see great and wonderful things? Yes, because: We have been blessed. We have been chosen. And we have been destined to be children of the most, high God. So be it.

Let us pray:
O Lord, we have so much to be thankful for this day. Open our eyes and help us to see all that You have given to us. Help us to see that we are indeed blessed, chosen and destined to be Yours. Help us to be thankful for Your abundantly gracious gift of Jesus Christ. And let us share that it is Your will that all shall come to Him and receive that abundantly gracious gift, as well.

And now, this evening and next Thursday, as we head to the Thanksgiving table let us remember that all good things come only from You. And in knowing that, open our eyes and hearts to the ways we can best share the good news with others. In the name of Jesus Christ we pray. Amen.

Christ Is Coming

Matthew 24:36-44
"But about that day and hour no one knows, neither the angels of heaven, nor the Son, but only the Father. For as the days of Noah were, so will be the coming of the Son of Man. For as in those days before the flood they were eating and drinking, marrying and giving in marriage, until the day Noah entered the ark, and they knew nothing until the flood came and swept them all away, so too will be the coming of the Son of Man. Then two will be in the field; one will be taken and one will be left. Two women will be grinding meal together; one will be taken and one will be left. Keep awake therefore, for you do not know on what day your Lord is coming. But understand this: if the owner of the house had known in what part of the night the thief was coming, he would have stayed awake and would not have let his house be broken into. Therefore you also must be ready, for the Son of Man is coming at an unexpected hour.

Today is the first Sunday of a new season, a season of anticipation, a season of hope and waiting, a time of preparation as we look forward to the birthday of the Christ-child. Today begins the season of Advent that points to an extraordinary moment, the birth of Christ which includes much more than just Christmas morning. Understanding that moves us away from the sentimental feelings we normally have for Christmas and into its true meaning, its extraordinary meaning. You see, the birth of Christ affected the whole universe for all eternity. The eternal God was incarnated in a man named Jesus. Jesus is God's Word-story in the flesh. And like all stories it has a beginning and will someday have an ending, a completion.

So, when we think about the Advent season we see that it's not only about the birth of Christ, but it's also about His second coming. In that sense our whole lives are a time of Advent, a time of waiting. Advent is a time of preparation, too. It is a time when we look back examining Israel's expectation of the long-awaited Messiah, and it is a time to look forward to the day when Jesus will return.

Let us pray: May the words of my mouth and the meditations of each of our hearts be acceptable in Your sight, O God, our Rock and our Redeemer. Amen.

We do not know when that long anticipated event shall occur, but hopefully, we will stay prepared. And we can do that by doing two things, seeking to bring our lives into tune with God and striving to live our lives boldly and without reservation for Him.

Jesus gave His disciples the example of Noah, when they started asking questions. Noah was in tune with God. His neighbors were not. Noah obeyed God and began preparing for the flood by building an ark in fair weather. Noah's neighbors must have thought he was crazy. But Noah knew what was about to happen. He was in tune. We need to be in tune, as well. A few weeks before Christmas, one mom asked her eight-year-old son, David, and two of his friends: "What Christmas songs are you learning in school this year?" And, David, looking down at his feet, replied, "Our teacher says we can't sing good enough. She's only going to let kids sing in the program who can carry a tune." David's mother could sense the hurt in her son's voice. She was hurt herself at the teacher's remark. And so she asked, "How'd you like to practice your song with me?" They began practicing the song their class would sing at the Christmas program, "It Came Upon the Midnight Clear." And as they practiced she began to think that perhaps the teacher was right. These boys could not carry a tune. That evening, after the children had gone to bed, she told her husband, "You never heard anything like it in your whole life. Never. You can't imagine what it was like!"

Her husband replied, "Oh, yes, I can, too. There are people, you know, who really can't carry a tune." "What's the use of trying to do what you can't do?" she exclaimed with a little exasperation. But, the next morning while shopping she bought two books on teaching music to children. They practiced from that afternoon until the night of the Christmas program. She adapted and invented "musical games to help teach the boys." She was patient with them. And, slowly, gradually, they began to sing on key, and were beginning to sound good. And on the night of the Christmas program David and his friends sang with the rest of the class. They were as good as all the rest. David no longer felt left out, thanks to the extra effort of his mother. In the weeks of practicing something else stirred inside of David. A few nights later his mother looked out the kitchen window to see David standing knee deep in snow. He just stood there looking toward the sky. When she stepped out David came running to her, "It's so still" he said in a hushed voice she had never heard before. "All those stars; look how they shine." Do you remember in the song "the world in solemn stillness lay?" And then, in his honest little-boy eyes his mother saw the miracle of an awakening soul.[102] David was truly in tune now. We need to make sure we are in tune with God, as well.

We can be prepared for Christmas, by seeking to bring our lives into tune with God. And we can be prepared for Christmas by living our faith boldly and without reservation. Britain's greatest blunder in World War I happened in a narrow strait of water in Turkey, the Dardanelles that connects the Aegean Sea to the Sea of Marmara and Constantinople. Sir Winston Churchill recommended that the British, the greatest fleet in the world at the time, sail up that straight of water, take Constantinople, and end the war. On March 18, 1915, the invasion began. The first day went perfectly but at the end of the day, largely out of fear of the risk and danger ahead, the admirals decided against Churchill's recommendation. They decided to pull back and take a more cautious approach. Historians agree this missed opportunity allowed the war to go on for three more years.

Ten years after the aborted invasion, Admiral Roger Keys sailed up the narrows into Constantinople. And when he arrived he said, "It would have been even easier than I thought! We simply couldn't have failed, and because we didn't try, another million lives were thrown away as the war went on for another three years."[103] The British missed their opportunity, and the consequences were not good. They missed it because they were paralyzed with fear and afraid of risks. They missed it and never had another one like it. Jesus never meant for His disciples to shrink back from the world in fear, but to walk confidently as ambassadors of His love. And so, we prepare for His coming by living our faith boldly and without reservation.

Eleanor Roosevelt wrote a Christmas story about a seven-year-old girl named Marta and her mother. Marta's father had been killed in World War I. She and her mother remembered the previous Christmas he had spent with them. And things just weren't the same now. They didn't really feel like celebrating. On Christmas Eve though, Marta asked her mother if she could light the one candle in the pantry that was left from last year's feast. "May I light it in the house so the light will shine out for the Christ Child to see His way," she asked. And Marta's mother said: "Well of course" and smiled. So Marta took out the candle and carefully placed it in a copper candlestick which had always held a lighted candle on Christmas Eve. And she wanted to see how far the light would shine in the night so she went outside. The wind was blowing around her; she could hardly stand up. She took two or three steps and looked back at the window. She could see the twinkling flame of the candle. While she stood watching it, she became conscious of a person in a dark coat standing beside her. She was not exactly afraid of this stranger, 'cause she was a brave little girl, but she felt a sense of chill creeping through her. Finally, the stranger spoke. "What are you doing here, little girl?" And Marta responded: "I came out to make sure that the Christ Child's candle would shine out to guide Him to our house."

"You don't really believe in any such legend, do you," asked the stranger. "That's silly. There is no Christ Child," he said. "That's just a story that's told for the weak. It's ridiculous to believe that a little child could ever lead the people of the world, a foolish idea," said the stranger. But that's what Marta had believed all her life and she wasn't going to change her belief now. Why, she had talked to the Christ Child herself. Marta then was beginning to feel very cold and she replied, "I am hoping the Christ Child will come and I am going in now, won't you come into the house with me?" The stranger seemed to hesitate a minute, but perhaps he decided it would be interesting to see the inside of such a humble home where there was such a simple faith. Marta's mother, who had been sitting by the fire knitting, was still there, yes, but in her arms now was a baby and around the two of them a curious light shone, and Marta knew that the Christ Child would come.[104] A simple story, but filled with truth. He is coming.

When Jesus came the first time, He came as a baby in a manger in an obscure village. Nobody much knew or cared except Mary and Joseph, some shepherds and angels. But when He comes the second time, all will see Him and recognize that something spectacular has happened. Jesus tells His disciples: *There will be signs in sun and moon and stars, and upon the earth.*[105] There will be signs and circumstances reverberating through the entire universe. There will be signs, Jesus says, things which will cause people to fear. And when the signs come, Christians can take comfort in knowing that it is all in God's plan that *"their redemption is drawing near."* God will never leave us. His Love will not be defeated and nothing will be able to separate us from that Love. Now, God never promised a life free from trial. God never promised that life would be easy or that everything would go our way. God never even promised that we wouldn't be ridiculed for our faith in Him. Marta realized that at a very young age. But, God did promise that He would always be with us, no matter what. That's the Hope of Christmas.

Time began anew with the birth of Jesus. The Incarnation established a new situation for humanity in the cosmos. With the birth, the death and the resurrection of Jesus Christ a whole new world was created. And when anyone is united with Christ, even today, there is a newness, a newness where Christ rules as Lord, where the Holy Spirit continues to bring New Life, where Love is the rule. I suspect that if we had been there at the birth of Christ, we would have seen and heard things that would be hard to reconcile with modern science. But, that is not the point. The point is that when Jesus was born the whole course of history was changed. The birth of Jesus made possible not just a new way of understanding life, but a new way of living life. Since His birth, countless people have been filled with His Spirit. Countless have been touched by Him; they have been caught up in His life and have found themselves in deep and private ways healed and transformed. He is indeed the long-expected One. Through Him, God brings light into our darkness. And through belief in Him, we are made whole and given New Life. He is our Salvation. He is the Good News of God. And so even today, we wait with anticipation, not only, for the birthday of our Lord, but also, for His return. Amen.

An Extraordinary Obedience

<u>Matthew 1:18-25</u>
Now the birth of Jesus the Messiah took place in this way. When his mother Mary had been engaged to Joseph, but before they lived together, she was found to be with child from the Holy Spirit. Her husband Joseph, being a righteous man and unwilling to expose her to public disgrace, planned to dismiss her quietly. But just when he had resolved to do this, an angel of the Lord appeared to him in a dream and said, "Joseph, son of David, do not be afraid to take Mary as your wife, for the child conceived in her is from the Holy Spirit. She will bear a son, and you are to name him Jesus, for he will save his people from their sins." All this took place to fulfill what had been spoken by the Lord through the prophet: "Look, the virgin shall conceive and bear a son, and they shall name him Emmanuel," which means, "God is with us." When Joseph awoke from sleep, he did as the angel of the Lord commanded him; he took her as his wife, but had no marital relations with her until she had borne a son; and he named him Jesus.

An elementary school class was putting on a Christmas play which included the story of Mary and Joseph coming to the inn. In that class, was one little boy who wanted very much to be Joseph. But when the parts were handed out he was assigned to be the Inn Keeper instead. He was very bitter about this. So during all the rehearsals he kept plotting what he might do the night of the performance to get even with his rival. Finally, the night of the performance, Mary and Joseph came walking across the stage. They knocked on the door of the inn, and the Inn Keeper opened the door and asked them gruffly what they wanted. Joseph answered: "We'd like to have a room for the night."

Suddenly the Inn Keeper threw the door open wide and said: "Great, come on in and I'll give you the best room in the house." For a few seconds poor little Joseph didn't know what to do, and a long silence ensued. Finally though, thinking quickly on his feet, he looked in past the Inn Keeper, first to the left and then to the right and said: "No wife of mine is going to stay in a dump like this. Come on, Mary, let's go to the barn." And once again the play was back on track.[106] Little Joseph knew his role well, that of caring for Mary.

Let us pray: May the words of my mouth and the meditations of each of our hearts be acceptable in Your sight, O God, our Rock and our Redeemer. Amen.

In today's passage we hear of some of the things that preceded Mary and Joseph's arrival in Jerusalem. We hear that Joseph cared deeply for Mary. We hear that he risked his own reputation to protect hers. But there was something more than just a deep love for Mary. There was something more in Joseph's heart and that was an even deeper love for his God. Before the angel Gabriel spoke to Joseph in a dream, he was sent to a town in Galilee called Nazareth, to a virgin whose name was Mary. Mary was perplexed by the angel's appearance and by his greeting, when he said to her: *Do not be afraid, Mary, for you have found favor with God. And now, you will conceive in your womb and bear a son, and you will name Him Jesus. He will reign over the house of Jacob forever, and of His kingdom there will be no end.* Mary said to Gabriel: *"How can this be, since I am a virgin?"* And he responded: *The Holy Spirit will come upon you, and the power of the Most High will overshadow you; therefore the child to be born will be holy; He will be called Son of God.* This prophesied the birth of Jesus of Nazareth.

You know, God must have been extremely careful in selecting Mary. He must have seen qualities in her which allowed Him to know that she was well suited for this important role.

He probably knew she would be frightened by the appearance of the angel and perplexed by His message. But He also must have known that she had the potential within her to respond: *Behold, I am the handmaiden of the Lord; let it be to me according to Your word.* I mean, why else would God have chosen Mary to become the Mother of the Messiah if He didn't see within her the great potential of obedience? Mary's response is that of the perfect submission to God. In fact, we might say that Mary is a model for all of us. Literally, she made the decision to lay down her life for God's purposes. Mary was a young teenage girl of extraordinary obedience.

But there was someone else, as well, an almost invisible person who would contribute as much as Mary did. The man's name was Joseph and he had been called by God to carry out a very important task. But unlike Mary, he's not center stage. He doesn't have a leading role. He's not the bandleader or the drum major who stands in the limelight for all to see. No, he's pretty much invisible and hardly anyone talks of him. They barely speak his name. He appears for a time and then vanishes from the stage of human history. We all know Mary. She has high visibility. We know of Elizabeth and Zechariah, the parents of John the Baptist. We know of shepherds who kept their flocks by night. We know even of the notorious Herod who issued the decree that all baby boys under two years of age be slaughtered on sight. We know of all the cast and crew of the great Christmas pageant. But Joseph, who is he? Well, he's obscure. He's quiet. He's behind the scenes, maybe, too invisible for our liking. We really don't know a whole lot about him, except that he obediently takes Mary to be his wife and helps to raise and protect God's son, Jesus.

Joseph, first and foremost, was a man of substance. We know that because he accepts his role and carries out his responsibilities even when the whole world seemed to be against him. He is there for God and for Mary. He quietly and obediently responds to God's will and eventually, he leads Mary and Jesus to safety in Egypt.

Joseph was a man of substance even when he was under enormous pressure. In a culture that valued the sanctity of virginity before marriage, he would immediately come under great suspicion by those around him. Many thought that both he and Mary had broken their premarital vows. She was pregnant, by the Holy Spirit, of course, but who would have believed that? A much greater peril, though, was this: What was in the mind of Joseph himself. What would he think? How would and how could he believe Mary's story? He could have easily put her away. He could have easily written her off, but because he was a man of substance because he trusted in God and believed that his dream was a revelation from God. He decided to take Mary to be his wife. And he made a decision to help raise the child she was carrying.

Think about it, Joseph is just a minimum wage worker, a carpenter, trying to take care of those he loved most. He's not fighting for an authoritative role in the synagogues. He's not a member of Herod's imperial guard. He's not a prophet or a priest. Not a prince or a magistrate. Not a gladiator or a Roman terminator. His life was that of a very low profile. But, as we see here, you don't have to have a high profile or great visibility to be a person of substance. What made Joseph a great man of substance was the fact that he made the right choices amid great odds and allowed the Spirit of the Lord to guide him in making a decision that would change the world for ever. Joseph was a man of great substance in God's eyes because of the decisions he made. He was a man of substance, but there was even more. He was also a man of presence. He was present. He was at the right place at the right time. You don't hear his words, Matthew doesn't record a single word that Joseph utters except the fact that he names the baby Jesus, but you see the imprints of his presence through what he does. He had the confidence to be who God had made him to be. He didn't speak many words, but when Mary needed him, he was there.

One man tells the story of how he lost his wife, and how he was terribly distraught. His close friend came by. They walked by the seaside and the man poured out his heart to him. They walked the bustling streets of New York and his friend listened and provided a presence that helped the man get through the biggest loss of his life. Presence doesn't always mean words. What's more important than that is the ability and willingness to be there for another in their time of need. Joseph was a quiet man. And his quiet and gentle spirit allowed him to be present with Mary in a world that was very hostile to unwed mothers. Joseph was there for Mary. Who waited on her hand and foot when she was carrying that baby? Who found the place for them to stay on that cold, windy night when most of the homes were full? Who stoked the fires and bailed the hay? Who ran the errands and brought them food to eat? Who kept watch when Herod's soldiers were running wild in the streets looking to kill the first two-year-old they saw who, looked, anything like a messiah? Who was there at daybreak and midnight? Who buttered the bread and poured the coffee? Who turned the straw, counted the sheep, and watered the trough for the animals after the baby was born? Joseph was present; he was there in body, mind and spirit, helping God do a new thing through His Son, Jesus. In this story, we see vividly, that it's not a persons' visibility but their availability that counts in the eyes of God. Joseph's willingness to take Mary as his wife turned her cross into a crown and helped God give humanity a Savior.

Joseph was a man of substance and a man of presence. And Matthew reveals that he was also a man of action. He writes: *After his first dream about the birth of the child, Joseph did what the angel of the Lord had commanded him and took Mary to be his wife.*[107] And later, we hear that an angel of the Lord appears to Joseph again and tells him to take the child and escape to Egypt.[108] Which, of course he does. As a man of action he did what God told him to do. And after being in Egypt some time, an angel of the Lord appears a third time and tells him to take the child back to Israel. Again, he got up and took the child and his wife back to Israel.[109]

The scriptures don't record all the deeds of Joseph, but, from what we do read, we see that he was a man of action. It is clear that the three actions recorded there, were very, very important, perhaps, three of the most important acts in history. Sometimes it's not the amount of things that we do, but what we do when the moment requires it. Action on our part, when God calls for action, can bring about the most amazing things in this world. Joseph didn't pass decrees or implement legislation. He wasn't known for the enormity of his deeds. But the fact that he acted on the entreaties of God at a critical time made him a great, great man. Think about it. Joseph didn't have high visibility. In fact, we might say he had no visibility compared to others in the Bible. But he had three things, which made him extraordinary. He was a man of substance. He was a man of presence. And he was a man of action.

In other words: You don't have to be seen to be visible. You just need to have substance in the things you have been called by God to do. You don't have to be heard to be visible. You just need to have a presence in all things vital to God. You don't have to do a lot to be visible. You just need to take action in times of critical decision-making. A low profile does not mean lack of substance, lack of presence, or lack of action. It just means that God can and will use anyone who is open to being used by Him. Joseph changed the course of human history by playing a supporting role. Because of his humble obedience, the baby Jesus was born safely in Bethlehem. Mary was the first key human player in the birth of God's Son and Joseph was the second.

Someone once said: A saint is simply a person to whom God has given strength to take His basic commandment, to love God and others, with utter seriousness, to understand it profoundly, and to exert every effort to carry it out. Who could doubt that Mary and Joseph loved God and others? Mary certainly took His Word seriously, didn't she? Why else would she have consented to God's request in the first place?

And Joseph, well without him, Mary and the baby didn't have much of a chance in a society that normally stoned a woman to death for being "with child" and no husband. The two of them must have received an abundant measure of grace to have offered themselves to God, as they did.

Maybe God has some special work for you this Advent season. What if you decided to pray fervently, asking God to open your heart and mind to the work He has for you during this time of waiting? What kind of work does God have in mind for you as you give of your substance, your presence, and your action? Who knows? Well, God does and He's waiting for your response. Will you be obedient like Joseph and Mary? Will you make the decision to answer God's call? Let your response be like that of Joseph and Mary. Let it be that of an extraordinary obedience, because you, like them, trust in God and His ability and willingness to use your life, today, for His glory. Amen.

A Time to Leap for Joy

Luke 1:39-45
In those days Mary set out and went with haste to a Judean town in the hill country, where she entered the house of Zechariah and greeted Elizabeth. When Elizabeth heard Mary's greeting, the child leaped in her womb. And Elizabeth was filled with the Holy Spirit and exclaimed with a loud cry, "Blessed are you among women, and blessed is the fruit of your womb. And why has this happened to me, that the mother of my Lord comes to me? For as soon as I heard the sound of your greeting, the child in my womb leaped for joy. And blessed is she who believed that there would be a fulfillment of what was spoken to her by the Lord."

I'd like to begin this morning with a funny story about a Christmas program that went awry. It seems that there was once a pastor who had a great plan to illustrate the baby Jesus coming down from heaven. And the pastor asked one of the church leaders, Fred, to help. In preparation, he carefully attached a baby doll to an invisible fishing line, stringing it through hooks in the ceiling and across to Fred's fishing pole in the wings. This baby doll was to be the baby Jesus. As his sermon progressed, the pastor would come to the words, "and Jesus came down from heaven that night and into the manger of Bethlehem." Fred was to take that cue to lower the "baby Jesus" into the manger waiting below. The cue came, and the baby was lowered only to stop precariously swinging ever so slightly about 4 or 5 feet above the crib. And there the baby Jesus hung suspended for ever so long above the manger. The pastor repeated the cue, hoping Fred would let out more line, but to no avail. What the good pastor could not know was that Fred had come to the end of his fishing line.

So there baby Jesus hung, floating above the manger, his intended destination. Finally realizing what had happened, the pastor decided to take matters into his own hands, as pastors often do. He walked over, grabbed baby Jesus dangling there and pulled him toward the crib. Naturally, he pulled Fred from the wings as well, fishing pole still in hand. Embarrassed beyond belief, Fred rushed back out of sight, only to yank the baby Jesus back toward the heavens with him.[110] Now thankfully, there is no flying baby in the original Christmas story. However, there is a leaping one.

Let us pray: May the words of my mouth and the meditations of each of our hearts be acceptable in Your sight, O God, our Rock and our Redeemer. Amen.

After the angel Gabriel appears to Mary to tell her she would bear a son, Mary, excited and scared, goes to visit her relative Elizabeth, in the hill country of Judea. Mary was determined to see her older relative, even though it was a difficult journey for her. Now, Elizabeth was married to a man named Zacharias. You remember Zacharias; he was a priest. And he and Elizabeth were advanced in years, and had no children. But the angel Gabriel came to Elizabeth, too and announced that she would bear a son who was to be named John. John would be a prophet like Elijah and would fulfill Malachi's prophecy that told of a special messenger who would come and *"prepare the way for the Lord."[111]* When Mary arrived at Elizabeth's home, Elizabeth was in her sixth or seventh month of pregnancy. And that's when a very interesting thing happened. Luke tells us that when Elizabeth heard Mary's greeting, the baby leaped in her womb, and Elizabeth was filled with the Holy Spirit. And in a loud voice she exclaimed to Mary: *"Blessed are you among women, and blessed is the child you will bear!... As soon as the sound of your greeting reached my ears, the baby in my womb leaped for joy."*

Speaking of excitement let me share with you a poem appearing in *Christianity Today* called, "Sharon's Christmas Prayer." It was about a little five-year-old girl who was very sure of the facts about Mary and Joseph. And she recited them, the facts, with slow solemnity, convinced that every word was a revelation. She said: "They were so poor they had only peanut butter and jelly sandwiches to eat. And they went a long way from home without getting lost. The lady rode a donkey, the man walked, and the baby was inside the lady. They had to stay in a stable with an ox and an ass, and then she giggled. But the Three Rich Men found them because a star lighted the roof. Shepherds came and you could pet the sheep but not feed them. Then the baby was borned. And do you know who he was?" Her quarter eyes inflated to silver dollar size. "The baby was God." And she jumped in the air, whirled around, dove into the sofa, and buried her head under the cushion, which of course, is the only proper response to the Good News of the Incarnation. Can't you just envision that? After telling the Christmas story, she jumped in the air, whirled around, dove into the sofa, and buried her head under the cushion. Wow! Christmas was an exciting time for her as it should be for us, because Christmas is about God coming into our world. The Christmas story is an exciting story. No wonder the baby leaped.

Blessed are you, Mary, blessed are you among women. And blessed is the fruit of your womb Jesus. And blessed are all those who hear Him, believe Him, and follow Him in the ways of peace and justice and love," exclaimed Elizabeth. And then from Mary and Elizabeth's conversation comes a song, a reflection of Hannah's song from the Old Testament book of 1 Samuel. The Magnificant, as it is called, came from the lips of a simple, teenage girl who grew up in the obscure village of Nazareth in what is now northern Israel. The angel Gabriel announced that she had been chosen to be the mother of the long-awaited Messiah. And Mary with insight far too profound for a simple teenager declared the impact that her son would have upon the world. She announced two distinct things in the Magnificant, which Jesus would instigate and activate.

She spoke of these things in the past tense, as if they had already happened. A young peasant girl gave birth to a ground-breaking idea that would become the pattern for all others. Let's look at the verses that define this. The first radical thing that Mary spoke of was spiritual in nature. We read: *"He has scattered the proud in the thoughts of their hearts."* In other words, God has confused the proud and arrogant of heart. He has taken away their peace of mind. A pastor from Chicago was on a plane one day when the man seated beside him struck up a conversation. Upon finding out that he was a minister, the man said with a proud and arrogant heart: "Well, I believe in God but I don't affiliate with any church. Don't really think I need it. Sure, I make some mistakes but I live respectably and give to charities. I wouldn't hurt a soul on purpose. I believe that God will accept me on that basis." Then the pastor took out a legal pad and said, Let's make a grading scale for all people, from one to ten, with ten being just about perfect. And then he asked: Who do you think are the two best people in the world? And the man thought for a moment and said: Mother Teresa and Billy Graham. Okay, the pastor said. But we must allow them to place *themselves* on our chart. Each of them has said: I am a sinner and have no chance of salvation unless it is a gift to me from Christ. So, by their own admission, they deserve to be down near the bottom of the chart. Now, my next question is: Where should we put you on the chart? Do you want to be above Mother Teresa and Billy Graham? And the man thought for a while and then replied: Well, if they're not perfect enough to get into heaven, I guess I'm in worse shape than I thought. Then the pastor drew a cross right across the middle of the chart. Underneath that cross he wrote these words from 1 John 2: *But if anyone does sin, we have an advocate with the Father, Jesus Christ the righteous, and He is the atoning sacrifice for our sins.* And underneath that he drew a dotted line and said to the man: Just sign here if you would like to be covered by the sacrifice of Christ. Then you can be sure of going to heaven. And the man signed on the dotted line.[112]

Now, of course this would also have to involve the proper desire of the man's heart and not just the physical signing on the dotted line. There has to be a connection between head and heart, which requires a certain amount of humility. The first thing Mary spoke of points to the fact that we have to banish all pride and spiritual self-sufficiency if we want to be covered by the sacrifice that Christ made on the cross for us.

The second thing that Mary spoke of was worldly in nature. We read: *"He has brought down the powerful from their thrones and lifted up the lowly."* You know, God is always overturning the world's social order. For example: He helped a band of Hebrew slaves defeat an Egyptian pharaoh. He took a humble shepherd boy, David, and made him Israel's greatest king. He took a murderer, Saul of Tarsus, and made him evangelist to the world. And when he sought a woman to be the mother of the Messiah, He chose a lower-class teenager from a little bitty country town. Think of that. God brings down kings and lifts up peasants. Is it because He values the peasant's life over the kings? No. Is it because He wants those who have no advantages to be given more? No. Well then why is it? Because, I think, He hates corruption. God does not mind a king being a king if that king is just. And He does not mind a peasant being poor so long as the powerful will help the less fortunate. God is not after a social equality. He is after hearts of justice and charity and love whether kings or peasants. To accomplish this He, at times, humbles the powerful and lifts up the lowly. And it is this reversal of fortunes that reminds us we are all equal before God. And that is part of the good news of Christmas. The Good News is that our God is a God of reversals and speaking of reversals. Think about this. God's good news sweeps away the world's bad news like a broom sweeps away dust. God brings hope in the midst of despair and healing in the midst of hurt. God brings peace in the midst of strife and comfort in the midst of grief. God brings companionship to the lonely and family to the forgotten. God brings power to the weak and justice for the oppressed. And most importantly, God brings to those humble in heart and mind New life in the midst of death.[113]

In other words, God comes to people who are in despair, who are hurting, under stress, grieving, lonely, forgotten, weak or oppressed. God comes to people who know they need God. And especially, God comes to those who are imprisoned by the human condition called sin, which really includes all of us.

Think about these things. The greatest leader of Israel, Moses, was told by God at the burning bush to remove his sandals for he was on holy ground because his sandals represented his sinfulness. The great prophet, Isaiah, confessed: "I am a man of unclean lips." The great Christian, Paul, confessed that he was "chief of sinners." You know what? It takes humility, it takes a laying aside of pride to be able to receive the gift that was offered on that first Christmas morn. And so in light of that let us all approach the manger this year, in a different way, in a way that will show that our hearts are truly humble before God.

Let us approach the manger in a way that will reveal that we adore Him and we are so thankful that our God is a God who did not merely survey the human situation from a safe distance, but He emptied Himself, laying aside His celestial robes to be clothed in the simple form of a human. God has come into the world. And His plan for the world continues to be fulfilled in the hearts of humble people everywhere even as we speak. And because of that Christmas should be a time when we all leap for joy.

Think about this for a moment: Divinity clothed Itself with dust, so that we who are made from dust will be able to enjoy eternity with God. Now that's exciting! God became flesh and dwelt among us. God was at work at the manger of Bethlehem offering a Salvation that would reconcile the world to God's own self. No wonder the baby, John, leaped for joy. Christmas is, indeed, a very exciting time, if you know, really know, deep down inside, really know, the true meaning of it. Christmas is a time to leap for joy. Amen.

From Presents to Presence

Luke 2: 8-20

In that region there were shepherds living in the fields, keeping watch over their flock by night. Then an angel of the Lord stood before them, and the glory of the Lord shone around them, and they were terrified. But the angel said to them, "Do not be afraid; for see--I am bringing you good news of great joy for all the people: to you is born this day in the city of David a Savior, who is the Messiah, the Lord. This will be a sign for you: you will find a child wrapped in bands of cloth and lying in a manger." And suddenly there was with the angel a multitude of the heavenly host, praising God and saying, "Glory to God in the highest heaven, and on earth peace among those whom he favors!" When the angels had left them and gone into heaven, the shepherds said to one another, "Let us go now to Bethlehem and see this thing that has taken place, which the Lord has made known to us." So they went with haste and found Mary and Joseph, and the child lying in the manger. When they saw this, they made known what had been told them about this child; and all who heard it were amazed at what the shepherds told them. But Mary treasured all these words and pondered them in her heart. The shepherds returned, glorifying and praising God for all they had heard and seen, as it had been told them.

It was Christmas Eve, and the first of fourteen thousand people began streaming through the building's huge double doors. A beam of light shone down from above, as though from heaven itself, highlighting an elaborate nativity scene.

Marble angels gazed down upon the largest pipe organ in the world. And as people settled into their seats, the organist struck a chord that led the crowd in the singing of the first hymn: "O Come All Ye Faithful." Does that sound like a Christmas Eve Service at one of our big mega-churches? That's the impression we get, but actually it was an annual attraction in Philadelphia, in the early 1900's, that drew 1000's shoppers to a leading department store. Think about that. In contrast to the story we just heard, what happens in our stores today? Were your shopping trips this year a spiritual experience? Or were they better described as, just the sound of secular holiday music and children whining to go home?

Let us pray: May the words of my mouth and the meditations of each of our hearts be acceptable in Your sight, O God, our Rock and our Redeemer. Amen.

Christmas shopping is no fun anymore. Did you see on T.V. where people this year were lining up in front of shoe stores, camping out in the parking all night long, just to get into the store to buy the newest tennis shoe, the *Air Jordans,* before they were sold out? And in some places the police were even called in because of pushing and shoving among those who were waiting. They were afraid that a riot would break out. Does that sound like the Christmas spirit to you? What if? What if? What if it were still possible for Christmas shopping to be a spiritual experience? What if, we could somehow connect together the ritual of giving presents at Christmas time with the presence of Jesus Christ, the gift of God, Himself, with us? What if we could incorporate into the presents that we give to one another, the presence of Christ, the presence that the first shepherds must have experienced on that starry night so long ago?

Luke writes: *In that region, there were shepherds living in the fields, keeping watch over their flock by night. Then an angel of the Lord stood before them, and the glory of the Lord shone around them, and they were terrified.*[114]

What we have here is a combination of the darkness of the night and the brilliance of the luminous glory of the Lord that shone all around. The visible manifestation of the very power and presence of God Himself are caught up in the birth of the Christ-child. And not surprisingly, God's presence stirs up a great fear in the shepherds. But the angel urges them to trade their "great fear" for "great joy." Why? Well, because of the good news and the resulting peace on earth that comes with God's presence among us. The prophet Isaiah speaks of the forthcoming presence of God when he says: *Get up to a high mountain, O Zion... lift up your voice with strength, O Jerusalem... lift it up, do not fear; say to the cities of Judah. 'Here is your God!' See, the Lord GOD comes with might... He will feed his flock like a shepherd; he will gather the lambs in his arms... and gently lead the mother sheep.*[115] The long awaited Messiah, the Ruler of all rulers has been born. A great gift has been given to humankind.

What is the greatest gift you have ever received? A car, maybe a large sum of money, a long awaited child, or a spouse who loves you so unselfishly that you have to pinch yourself, every so often, to see if you are really awake? All of these things are very good. But none of them can come close to the gift that God offers to us through His Son. When God took on human flesh in the person of Jesus Christ, He offered to all of humanity the greatest gift of all. He offered the gift of Salvation, eternal life, God with us forever. It's a free gift to us, this gift of God, but like any other gift it has to be opened, to be received.

While visiting with an elderly woman, a pastor was asked to get a box of letters from the dresser drawer. And as she was getting the letters, she saw a beautiful quilt inside. And so she asked about it. Quickly, the elderly woman instructed her to take it out and look at it. What a masterpiece it was. She told the pastor that her grandmother had made the quilt as a wedding gift years earlier. And when asked why she didn't have it on her bed, she said, "Oh, well, it's just too beautiful to use."

This woman knew about the gift that her grandmother longed for her to enjoy, but she was afraid to open it, she was afraid to use it, and so, she tucked it away in a drawer for many years. In reality, she never truly received the gift. She knew in her mind that the quilt was beautiful, and she knew that her grandmother had designed it especially for her use, but she was not able to reap the benefits of it. She never experienced the beauty of the quilt in its fullness, as it was meant to be experienced. She only saw the outer wrapping, but never experienced the warmth it could bring. God's presence with us is sort of like that. We can go to church every week. We can read the Bible faithfully. We can hear the Christmas story over and over again. We can hear the story of God's salvation for us. But if we tuck it away in a drawer somewhere; if we only see the beauty of the outer wrapping and never invite Jesus Christ into our lives, into our daily existence, then we cannot reap the warmth of God's love and we cannot benefit from God's salvation offered so freely and so lovingly to us.

The gift of salvation, the presence of "Christ in us" and "with us" begins when we believe that He comes to redeem us, to cover our sins, so that we can stand before God, accepted and forgiven, and so that we can one day be ushered into God's eternal presence. When we receive the gift of Jesus Christ and truly believe that He came to take our place on Calvary, when we truly believe that through Christ, God accepts us just as we are, washes us clean and gives us new life, then, and only then, can we reap the benefits of God's gift to us. In other words, in order to benefit from God's gift, we must first receive.

There are many reasons why people choose not to receive God's gift of salvation. But the most common reason, I think, is that of thinking that a person must first get his or her life in order. Here's a modern day parable that might help. Early one morning fire broke out in a house on a narrow street. The alarm was sounded by a policeman on duty, but before the fire engines could get to the scene, flames were already leaping high into the air.

Suddenly a young man appeared at an upper window in his pajamas. Firemen quickly placed a ladder against the burning building. But to the frustration of all, he refused to come down, shouting back that he had to get dressed first. The firemen pleaded, "Come as you are! Come as you are!" but to no avail. From below they tried to climb the stairs, but were turned back as the wind fanned the flames into fury. When the rescuers tried to enter through a window, the heat and smoke forced them away. Suddenly the stairs gave way and the roof fell in. The man had waited too long and was buried beneath the ruins. How much greater tragedy awaits those who refuse to receive God's provision and safety in Christ because they want to get dressed up in the clothes of self-righteousness or religion. But the fact of the matter is that God doesn't require that we get dressed up for Him, but only that we come to faith in Christ, pajamas and all. It is not our ability to impress God or anyone else, but our availability to receive God's gift that counts.

Sometimes we get a little side-tracked at Christmas time. We get a little confused about what Christmas is all about. We begin to think that it all revolves around, a bounteous home cooked dinner, family gatherings, or giving the perfect gift, when in reality it is really about worshiping God in His house and celebrating the gift of Christ to us.

You know, Jesus talked about the spirit of a child many times. Once He said: *Truly I tell you, unless you change and become like children, you will never enter the kingdom of heaven. Whoever becomes humble like this child is the greatest in the kingdom of heaven.*[116] Children just naturally have the spirit of Christmas within them as seen in this next story. Caught up in the spirit and excitement of gift giving as only a three-year-old can be, a little girl picked up, examined, shook and tried to guess what was inside of every package. Then, in a burst of inspiration, she found a big red bow that had fallen off one of the gifts and held it on top of her head.

She looked up at her father with twinkling eyes and a beaming smile and said: "Look at me daddy, I'm a present." Children are indeed, presents, gifts from God. And that helps us understand the kind of God we have, He went so far as to be born into this world as a child. Love came down at Christmas. God's gift is real. God's eternal presence with us is for you and for me. Let's celebrate that together this year.

You know, thinking about all those people in line for the new *Air Jordans* what if, what if you had a chance to be there too? What if you turned to the person behind you, found out what shoes they were buying. Then what if you bought them, then turned and gave the shoes to them saying: Merry Christmas. God loves you. Do you think that might make shopping a spiritual experience for them and for you? Who knows what God might do with something like that! Maybe, it would start a chain reaction as others turned to those behind them and did the same. Gosh, maybe the whole crowd would be able to bask in the presence of Christ with them. That's what God would want for us. He would want us to bask in His presence with us. He would want us to bask in the gift of His salvation that comes only through belief in Jesus Christ, the: King of kings, Lord of lords, Prince of Peace, Almighty God and Savior.

Love came down at Christmas, but only a few perceived its coming. Have you perceived it? Does your heart long to be here every time the church doors are open? Have you truly perceived God's Love for you? In the final days of this year, don't tuck the greatest gift of all away in a drawer somewhere. Open it up. Receive God's gift and share it with others, by truly surrendering all areas of your life to Christ. Surrender the festivities you have planned to Him. Surrender your gatherings to Him. Surrender your New Years rituals to Him. Surrender 45 minutes on New Year's Day to Him. By doing so, you and those around you will then be blessed by the guest of honor Himself, Jesus Christ with you. Now that's a great way to close out a good year. So be it. Amen.

END NOTES

[1] National Hope Through Personal Holiness, Tony Beam, www.crosswalk.com

[2] Acts 4:32

[3] 2 Thessalonians 3:10

[4] Genesis 2:15

[5] Leonard Sweet, Jesus Manifesto

[6] Transformed, Billy D. Strayhorn, ChristianGlobe Networks, Inc.

[7] Amos 3:8

[8] Colossians 3:17

[9] Barbara Brokhoff, "Unusual, To Say The Least!

[10] ChristianGlobe Networks, Inc.

[11] Luke 23:34

[12] Luke 22:19

[13] Exodus 13:6-8

[14] Luke 22:19

[15] 1 Corinthians 11:24-26

[16] Matthew 6:34

[17] Luke 6:20-23

[18] As told by Dean Register in the Minister's Manuel, 1995, 339

[19] Brett Blair

[20] Donald L. Deffner, Seasonal Illustrations, San Jose: Resource, 1992, p. 89

[21] Donald L. Deffner, Seasonal Illustrations, San Jose: Resource, 1992, 88

[22] 'How Failure Breeds Success,' Jena McGregor, BusinessWeek, July 3, 2006

[23] Mark 6:7

[24] 2 Corinthians 12:7-10

[25] Michael in My God Story, compiled by Bob Coy; Fort Lauderdale, FL: Calvary Chapel Church, Inc., 2001, pp. 32-36.5

[26] Rev. Billy D. Strayhorn, "Is That All?"

[27] Max Lucado

[28] John 3:2

[29] John 3:7

[30] John 7:45-52

[31] John 19:39

[32] The Journal of the Rev. Charles Wesley, M.A.; London: Wesleyan Methodist Book-Room, 1849 n.d., 1:90-95

33 Nehemiah Curnock, ed. The Journal of the Rev. John Wesley, A.M.; London: The Epworth Press, 1938, 1:465-477

34 1 Corinthians 1:18

35 John 3:14

36 John 12:31-32

37 John 12:23-25

38 John 12:32

39 Qur'an 2.087

40 Sura 4:157

41 John 12:27

42 Sura 5:116

43 Sahih Muslim hadith, Book #25, 025:5339: Chapter 004

44 Qur'an 5.017

45 Qur'an 17.111

46 Matthew 5:44

47 Matthew 10:16

48 Heaven, Randy Alcorn

49 Thich Nhat Hanh

50 John 12:23-32

51 Jeremiah 31:31

52 Jeremiah 31:31

53 Jeremiah 31:33

54 Jeremiah 31:34a

55 Isaiah 53:3

56 Matthew 26:26-28

57 John 1:4

58 John 1:5

59 John 12:32

60 Revelation 21:5

61 Isaiah 65

62 Matthew 19:28

63 Matthew 5:5

64 Randy Alcorn, Heaven, pp. 17-18

65 Revelation 21:1-2

[66] Revelation 21:3

[67] 1 Corinthians 3:12-14

[68] Philippians 4:8

[69] Revelation 22:2

[70] Randy Alcorn, Heaven

[71] Best Sermons 3, Harper & Row, 1990, pp. 49-50

[72] John 1:1-5; 9; 14

[73] Max Lucado, GOD CAME NEAR, p. 25

[74] Max Lucado, GOD CAME NEAR, p. 27

[75] Paul Harvey, The Man and the Birds

[76] Gordon MacDonald, The Life God Blesses, Thomas Nelson Publisher, 1994, Page 171-172

[77] Dr. Charles Hodge

[78] Paraphrased from 'The Answer's in Your Hands,' in William J. Bausch, *A World of Stories for Preachers and Teachers,* Mystic, Connecticut: Twenty-Third Publications, 1999, pp. 219-220

[79] 101 Things To Do During A Dull Sermon by Tim Sims and Dan Pegoda

[80] Mark 2:18-22

[81] John 10

[82] Interview by Tiffany Rose in the London Independent, excerpted in The Week August 19, 2005, p.12

[83] Mark 6:17

[84] Mark 6:18

[85] Matthew 19:9 (The Voice)

[86] Note on Matthew 19:9 (The Voice)

[87] 1 Corinthians 7:15

[88] Book of Discipline, 2004

[89] Book of Discipline, 2004

[90] Revelation 21

[91] Traditional

[92] Charles Swindoll

[93] See John Powell, Through the Eyes of Faith, Tabor Publishing, Allen, Texas 1992, pp. 60-61

[94] Rev. Brett Blair

[95] Today in the Word, March, 1990

96 Ruth Preston Schilk, Who Touched Me

97 William J. Gaither

98 Jim & Doris Morentz, MINISTER'S ANNUAL PREACHING IN 1989; Nashville:
Abingdon Press, 1988

99 LAUGH CONNECTIONS, Vol. No. 3 Summer, 1991, P.4

100 Catholic Digest

101 Joseph B. Clower, Jr. Cited in Sam J. Ervin, Jr., HUMOR OF A COUNTRY
LAWYER, Chapel Hill: University of North Carolina Press, 1983

102 Dorothy Canfield Fisher, 'The Night the Stars Sang,' THE GUIDEPOSTS
CHRISTMAS TREASURY, Carmel, NY: Guidepost Associates, 1972, pp. 3

103 William Manchester,THE LAST LION: WINSTON SPENCER CHURCHILL, Vol. I,
Boston: Little, Brown & Company, 1989

104 Collected Sermons, King Duncan, Dynamic Preaching, 2005, modified

105 Luke 21:25-28

106 Adapted from a story by John Simmons

107 Matthew 1:24

108 Matthew 2:13

109 Matthew 2:19-22

110 Pastor Dan Mangler

111 Luke 1:17; Mal. 3:1

112 Bill Hybel/ Willow Creek Church

113 David E. Leininger

114 Luke 2:8-9

115 Isaiah 40:9-11

116 Matthew 8:3-4

Proof

Made in the USA
Charleston, SC
03 January 2011